UP
FROM
APATHY

WITHDRAWN

UP
FROM
APATHY

A Study of
Moral Awareness
& Social Involvement

RICHARD A.
HOEHN

Abingdon Press
Nashville

UP FROM APATHY

Copyright © 1983 by Abingdon Press

Library of Congress Cataloging in Publication Data

HOEHN, RICHARD A., 1936–
  Up from apathy.
  Includes bibliographical references and index.
  1. Ethics.   2. Social ethics.   3. Social action.
  I. Title.
  BJ1012.H63   1983   172'.1   83-7057

ISBN 0-687-43114-X

The scripture quotation on page 139 is from the Revised Standard Version of
the Bible, copyrighted 1946, 1952, © 1971, 1973 by the Division of Christian
Education of the National Council of the Churches of Christ in the U.S.A., and
is used by permission.

Pages 113-16 of chapter 6 appeared in altered form in "Combating Racism:
Touch and Tell" by Richard A. Hoehn, copyright 1982 Christian Century
Foundation. Reprinted by permission from the March 3, 1982 issue of *The
Christian Century.*

Pages 48, 61, 82, and 120 contain selections from Edward A. Tiryakian's
chapter "Sociology and Existential Phenomenology" in *Phenomenology and
the Social Sciences,* edited by Maurice Natanson, copyright 1973 by
Northwestern University Press.

MANUFACTURED BY THE PARTHENON PRESS AT
NASHVILLE, TENNESSEE, UNITED STATES OF AMERICA

To
my parents
Albert C. Hoehn
and Mary Rieger Hoehn

CONTENTS

PREFACE

Every inquiry aims at some good, wrote Aristotle. The goal of this study has been to discover how people become involved in social change activities. This aim fits inside another which is primarily pedagogic—to determine how in a free society people might be educated and motivated to choose public participation in behalf of the human community.

Evidences of avoidance and apathy can be heard almost daily, especially with gallows humor about the impending nuclear holocaust: "When the warning comes, I plan to rush to Neiman Marcus and go out in style." The newspaper quotes a farmer whose property borders ICBM silos: "I know that we would be the first hit, but there is nothing you can do about it." We even hear: "I do not want to think about it."

This study consists of phenomenological reflections based on interviews of eighty-seven people, aged nineteen to seventy-four, who believe they can effect some measure of justice in a troubled world. The title, *Up from Apathy*, echoes Booker T. Washington's autobiographical *Up from Slavery*. The chains that bind us—apathy and its connecting links (greed, privatism, insensitivity, and hopelessness)—are more subtle because they are invisible. The people whom we have interviewed see a vision of a good society and invest part of their life substance working to give birth to it. The opportunity I have had to share in their lives has been felicitous indeed. I am thankful.

The research participants live in places as varied as Cuernavaca, Detroit, Washington, San Francisco, and the Fort Worth-Dallas area. Sixty-eight are white—of those, thirty-five are male and thirty-three female. Twelve blacks and eight Hispanic-Americans were interviewed. They include lawyers, homemakers, engineers, ministers, persons who work in community agencies, politicians, physicians, teachers, reporters, and students. The names used in the text are pseudonyms.

The interviews were aided by a grant from the Texas Christian University Research Foundation. The Association of Theological Schools, Brite Divinity School, and Texas Christian University provided funds, released time, and other less tangible forms of support.

Pages 113-116 originally appeared in altered form in *The Christian Century* 99.7 (March 3, 1982). Some of the ideas presented here appeared earlier in *Academy* 36.4 (December, 1979) and in *Consensus* 6.3 (July, 1980).

Tim Mabbott, Randy Hill, Marilyn Walker, Louis Eason, Carl Schanche, and I conducted the interviews. Betty Belton, Iris Valdez, Ann Chambers, and Leah Flowers typed various versions of the manuscript. Gibson Winter, Martin Marty, Richard Zaner, and Alvin Pitcher inspired, influenced, and informed me in many ways both personal and professional. Among the many people who provided helpful comments on drafts of the manuscript are June O'Connor, Terry Tekippe, E. Joyce Nebel, Jean Giles-Sims, Eugene Kile-Smith, Edward Vacek, Claudia Camp, and Skip Johnson. Cindy Johnson assisted in compiling the index. I am also very grateful to Patricia Behm Hoehn, Christine J. Hoehn, Thomas A. Hoehn, Karen E. Hoehn, Benjamin D. Hoehn, Gwyn Nolan, George and Marjorie Procter-Smith, Margie Schanche, the Ken Stoyers, and the members of my house church for their loving presence with me.

R.A.H.

INTRODUCTION: INSIDE THE ROOMS

Many good-hearted people who are moral in their personal lives, and who would help a needy friend, do not respond to larger public dimensions of human need. Though their core values affirm "love your neighbor," the bounds of neighborliness are rather tightly drawn. They seem unaware of the suffering of people who are strange to them—or perhaps they are aware, but for one reason or another do not act on that awareness.

This is a study of the experiences that lead some people to become aware and involved. The experience triggering this study occurred when the late John Howard Griffin spoke to a class I was teaching. His remarks brought into focus a host of questions that had been raised in graduate school at the University of Chicago and in my own coming to awareness and political activation.

It had been a pleasant surprise to learn that Griffin, author of *Black Like Me* and other works, lived but two blocks from my home in Fort Worth. In the early sixties his book had helped open my eyes to racism in America. I was delighted when he consented to speak to the class. It was not easy for him; illness had impaired his mobility. But he was extraordinarily gracious. After a brief presentation, he called for questions. A student asked why Griffin, a white, had blackened his skin to travel through the South as a black. Griffin answered:

I was born of an old southern fundamentalist family from Georgia. I had the kind of upbringing that society gave us those early years, which gave us the illusion that we didn't have a prejudiced bone in our body; we barely learned to hate.

I was very unhappy with the educational system in this country, and when I was sixteen I went to France. I was there until France fell.

I was in the French Underground smuggling Jewish people out of Germany from 1939 to 1940 and that was, of course, the first real awakening that I had to what racism was all about. It was a devastating shock to me to find that our preoccupation with the Hitler rationale had been merely intellectual.

I am ashamed to say that I made no connection between the reasoning we did where Jewish people were the victim group, and the same kind of reasoning I had been brought up with concerning a different victim group—the black people.

It was a tremendous kind of shock to me because we were intellectually discussing the great intellectual preoccupation of students in France just prior to the beginning of World War II, and we argued the pros and cons of the great change. I think the eye-opener was the night just before the fall of France. We had managed to get quite a few Jewish persons out of Germany and put them on boats to England. This time we had to have special kinds of papers to move any more over the age of fifteen, so we were caught with these families and no way to get them farther.

I was only one of two people in that area who was doing this kind of work. It was my task for this night to go and tell them that we were not going to succeed. We didn't have skills of forging papers. It was going into those rooms where we had them hidden that the whole thing, which has haunted me ever since in my work in this country, hit me square in the face. I went into the room where the mothers and fathers and children were hidden. I didn't have to tell a single one of those families that they were not going to succeed. They told me that it was all over; they said the first thing the Germans would do is to round them up and ship them back to Germany. Then they asked me to do a heartbreaking thing. They asked me to take their children, because we could move children under the age of fifteen.

And suddenly you were sitting in those rooms and you became aware of the fact that there are only two people in the world that knew who was in those rooms, myself and my teammate. Suddenly all this intellectual preoccupation we had was simply washed away because we were in the presence of a massive human tragedy—the tragedy of parents who loved their children and were giving their children away to someone they hardly knew, so at least the children would escape the camp.

I realized that I could go outside of those rooms, and I would go a block in any direction and could find a person who considered himself perfectly decent who had no idea of the reality inside those rooms. He might begin to rationalize and justify the racism which led to the tragedy inside of those rooms.

I have often in talks in this country wished that I could take people in such rooms. Because after *Black Like Me*, I became one of the few people who could circulate into the South and be completely hidden by black people.

And so it became my task, along with many other blacks, to investigate the tragedy that was committed against black people. This was always done thus: one might be picked up and taken into Mississippi by black people and stay in the homes of black people in the day and travel at night, so that he wouldn't be seen.

You were constantly in the presence of the same kind of massive human tragedy in the homes where young people had been murdered. One instance was where an eight-year-old child had a rope thrown at her by some men who were trying to frighten her. It was thrown around her neck, and she was dragged two blocks behind the car.

This kind of thing was going on in that kind of situation constantly. We were documenting all of this from the point of view of black people rather than take the opinion of whites in those communities who seemed not to know about the situation, or lied about it, or did not investigate it. And in these experiences, I was right back in those same kinds of rooms—rooms that were filled with grief-torn human beings. And when you go outside those rooms, you know that you can encounter people everywhere who considered themselves decent, and who would go right on rationalizing the racism, which led to the tragedy inside those rooms.

Griffin's tale, told to a hushed and respectful audience, resonated in the rooms of my mind, and hinted at answers to some nagging problems. The sixties and seventies had jarred my consciousness. In 1960 I didn't know there was a race problem in America. In 1963 I thought there was a black problem—by 1965 it was identified as a white problem. In 1970 the war in Vietnam was just another episode in American foreign policy. By 1974 it began to look more like a watershed in a long history of imperialistic interventions. And then came awareness of sexism, homophobia, world hunger, and the danger of nuclear disaster.

Through it all I was, in some sense, a moral person, or at least struggling hard to be moral. There were lacunae, and then unexpected inversions and great leaps forward. My perception of the world situation and my place in it would change radically. Meanwhile, many of my colleagues—even some ethicists— seemed to be doing business as usual, apparently not noticing the crisis proportions of world events. They seemed more bent on tuning rationality to ever higher and higher pitches that perhaps only they could hear, but paradoxically would not act on. The moral life seemed much different than their theories suggest. It is often messy, confused, incoherent—the contextual resolution of juxtaposing claims with the lingering knowledge that there are rarely unambiguous alternatives, because we live in a human world that is complex, dynamic, unfolding, and reflexive.

Who should do something about a world edging toward a long dark night, perhaps a new dark age? Not just the experts. Ordinary people somehow have to be empowered to create new possibilities in human history. Thus came this study of the moral lives of people who are socially and politically active. From them we can learn about the sources of moral concern and social involvement.

Griffin's remarks about the rooms in France and similar rooms in America suggest the metaphor "rooms"—the rooms inside our minds. The phenomenological method, with its emphasis on experience and consciousness, helps unlock doors to the rooms of people's inner moral lives—the symbolic places where they store up the memories that give vitality to their involvement. If we look inside the rooms of our minds, there is much there to be learned about the generative sources of moral awareness and social involvement—sources pointing toward a pedagogy for a world in the midst of a profound crisis that is not only economic and political, but finally moral.

Chapter 2 describes the experiences that brought people to an awareness of social problems. Griffin's experience inside those rooms in Germany and America had to do with the existential discovery of the depths of human suffering. Many of the awareness-shaping encounters in the interviews came through confrontations with human suffering. Sometimes it was the suffering of other people; sometimes it was the suffering of those interviewed.

The metaphors Griffin used to describe his experience cropped up in other interviews. "It shocked me," "it was an eye-opener," and "it hit me square in the face" are typical of the way the interview participants describe their experiences, and suggest something about the nature of moral conscious-ness. (At first, I had no intention of focusing on metaphors, but as they began to line up in rather tidy rows, it became obvious that to go anywhere but through them would be a detour.) Chapter 3 examines the coming-to-awareness experience through the metaphors used to describe it.

The change from unaware to aware can be thought of as a change in a person's frame of reference—the way in which one orients oneself to events. Chapter 3 examines the phenomenon of frames and frame changes. There are several possible change-of-frame experiences. There are triggering moments, moments in which everything comes into focus, moments of awakening, and moments with great emotional as well as cognitive meaning. Thus, Griffin describes how the discussion about the Jewish question was merely intellectual. It became a real and highly charged emotional event when he actually faced Jews on their way to the camps.

Whereas chapter 3 focuses on the structure of coming to awareness and change of frame, chapter 4 notes the moral dimensions of moments of awakening. Griffin's description is simultaneously a moral interpretation of the situation he confronted, and a normative judgment about what ought to be

done. Chapter 5 describes various elements in the activation experience—the move from concern to action. Chapter 6 presents further phenomenological reflections on the nature of moral consciousness based on the interviews but moving toward a normative theory of ethics. Chapter 7 consists of reflections on the interview process, suggesting that important experiences people can recall may have become the myths and symbols of their identity—the stories that they carry from the past to give meaning and direction to the present. We are, after all, our own memories and fantasies come alive.

Phenomenology

People who see the same event often report and interpret it differently, almost as though they had not seen the same thing. On the other hand, people who have differing experiences sometimes come to a common or shared view of reality. There is little, if any, conscious experience that remains uninterpreted. Frameworks of interpretation are fully as important to the viewer as the event or object being examined; they shape the way the event is appropriated.

The same holds true for research programs. The conclusions are as shaped by the interpretive theory brought to bear on them, as they are by the phenomena being studied. For example, those who use behavioral theories study behaviors, arrive at behaviorist conclusions, and recommend behaviorist policies. The phenomenological movement opens new doors in the social sciences, helping us to see phenomena in a fresh light. Phenomenology contributes both a methodology and an interpretive framework for this study.

Many philosophers seek an absolute ground of human certitude. Is there any certainty upon which an understanding of human existence might be based? Some say that there is certainty in nature—a tree is a tree, a rock can be counted on to be a rock. Phenomenologists suggest that appearances can be deceiving. The rock I step on as I cross the stream may turn out to be a turtle. The tree seen at a distance may turn out to be made of papier-mâché—part of a movie set. One cannot be absolutely sure about objects, but one can be certain that this object looks-like-a-tree, and that object feels-like-a-rock. One is existentially certain about the way one experiences things, if not always the things themselves.

The phenomenologist is interested in experience or experience-of phenomena. Thus, phenomenology is an apt method for the study of social involvement. I have investigated how people became socially involved by studying the experiences that have led people to choose involvement. The subject matter examined is experience of phenomena—not so much the events that change lives, as the way people perceive and recall these events. I have asked people to present their reality as they perceive it.[1]

Phenomenology also examines how experience is related to consciousness. The phenomenologist inquires first into the experience of something, then into the consciousness behind the experiencing.[2] Thus, I have studied the way experience leads to a change of consciousness, and then have stepped back to see what can be learned about moral consciousness itself.

Consciousness is not only a capacity for experiencing—it constitutes, structures, and assigns meaning to experienced reality. Phenomenologists describe consciousness as intentional. It reaches out and grasps objects and, in so doing, creates a certain kind of experience, with a distinctive meaning. If I do not notice the rock, I do not experience it; it is meaningless to me. But when my attention focuses on the rock, I not only see it, I endow it with meaning—as a hard object, an obstacle in my path, a sacred stone. This study of moments that quicken social involvement examines not only the events that happen to people, but the way these events are made meaningful. The interviews uncover those meaning-bearing experiences that are foundational to the respondents' concern and involvement.

Behavioral studies use a quantitative, objective approach to phenomena. They claim to look objectively at people's moral lives. They take the other person's moral life as an object of inquiry. The typical phenomenologist, by contrast, tries to penetrate into the subjective dimensions of human experience—to ascertain the way people themselves perceive and interpret their own moral lives. The phenomenologist is interested in presenting full qualitative descriptions—case studies—of these moral experiences and meanings, rather than statistical tables. The phenomenological researcher can bring a variety of research techniques to bear, but they are more like the techniques used by classical cultural anthropologists than those used by demographers. Specific techniques are tailored to the proximity, availability, and size of the group being studied.

The study that provided background for the present research grew out of phenomenologist Herbert Spiegelberg's experience of awakening-to-selfhood or what he called the I-am-me experience. As Spiegelberg reflected on this experience, he wondered whether other people had similar experiences. So he examined novels and autobiographies and discovered that many people had independently written about their own I-am-me experience. Jung describes his, which occurred at age eleven:

> It happened on my long walk to school . . . . There was a moment there in which I suddenly had the overwhelming feeling of having just come out of a dense fog with the consciousness: now I am me (jetzt bin ich *ich*). . . . At that moment I became an event to myself (geschah *ich mir*). Before that I was also around, but everything had merely taken place. This experience seemed to me enormously significant and novel. There was authenticity (*Autorität*) in it.[3]

Spiegelberg next administered questionnaires, which presented brief descriptions of the I-am-me experience, and asked respondents whether they could identify and describe similar experiences. Most could; their descriptions provided more research material. Spiegelberg divides the I-am-me experience into four different varieties, and concludes that the experience was "at least to some degree—one of the fundamental facts of human existence."[4]

Spiegelberg's order of inquiry illustrates the way in which a phenomenological social research project on a specific kind of experience might proceed. He began by reflecting on his own experience, and then compared that with published autobiographies. A questionnaire was used to discover whether the phenomenon was fairly widely experienced, and to gather additional descriptions. The questionnaire was not used to establish the reality of the I-am-me experience, but something of its general character. The experience was real, and hence valid, for Spiegelberg, even if no other person in human history had ever had it. The wider studies beyond his own introspection opened up some of the variety and complexity of the experience. The inquiry then moved from the empirical level of psychological investigation to an examination of the prior structures and processes of consciousness that made such an experience possible. Spiegelberg's order of inquiry parallels an order of inquiry suggested by Edmund Husserl (the founder of phenomenology) in *The Cartesian Meditations,* and thus gives shape to the present project.

The Participants

One way to discover why people are socially active is to interview them in the midst of their activism, as Kenneth Keniston did in his 1967 research on the anti-war protesters. In the *Young Radicals,* Keniston devotes about a dozen pages to the process by which latent radicals become activists.[5] However, it is not always possible to catch people in the midst of their activism, and there is no certainty that today's radical will not be tomorrow's banker. People who have dramatic change-of-consciousness experiences sometimes waver through a series of changes, ending up close to where they started. I wanted to know something about those people who had evidenced a commitment to social action over a period of time from several years to several score—people who had made lasting commitments to work toward a just and humane society.

Some were full-time activists, community organizers, and public officials. One claimed to have hijacked an airplane to Cuba, another to have organized with the Weather-people. Many were just concerned middle-class citizens who continually participate in efforts on behalf of the public good. A few non-activists were interviewed to lend contrast to the study. Because new occasions do teach new duties, a few of our activists have become backsliders since they were interviewed in 1975-76. Most, however, are doing as much or more now as they did then, though the specific activities have, in some cases, shifted. With only a few exceptions, I have interviewed people who are politically left of center. Some of my findings are presumably applicable not only to people at the opposite end of the spectrum but to all kinds of discoveries, awakenings, and activities. Other parts of the study apply only to those who basically are oriented to a liberal/radical view of justice and human community.

The interviews have been supplemented with the biographies or autobiographies that describe the change experiences of Margaret Sanger, Lincoln Steffens, Vladimir Nabokov, Pancho Villa, Booker T. Washington, Dorothy Day, Malcolm X, Dag Hammarskjöld, Nikki Giovanni, Angela Davis, Angelica Balabanoff, Frederick Douglass, James Forman, Henry David Thoreau, Franz Kafka, Betty Friedan, Jose Vasconcelos, Mother Teresa, Mahatma Gandhi, and some early labor movement leaders. Those chosen represent several racial and ethnic groups, and both sexes. Most were chosen for their activism—Nabokov, Hammarskjöld, and Thoreau were chosen because of their ability to explore and articulate inner experiences.

Newspaper and magazine accounts of awareness and activation experiences of people whose names will not be remembered—and others whose names stand a better chance, like Jane Fonda and Daniel Ellsberg—were clipped. The correlation between the experiences reported in the interviews and those recorded in print was extraordinarily impressive.

The interview process is excellent for eliciting people's interpretations of the experiences that have shaped their identities. It makes sense to listen to how they express their impressions of the moral life—the language they use, the variety of experiences they trace, and the symbols they project in expressing self-understanding. Over the years of this study, I have had many experiences in listening to everyday conversations that confirm the interpretations presented here. In addition, persons who have read drafts of the manuscript have commented, "Yes, that's the way it was for me, too." We re-interviewed four of the participants several years later and found that they presented the same or functionally similar experiences as in the first interview.

Additional confirmation came via a newspaper article. Carl was interviewed by a journalist, and parts of his life story went into a full-page personal profile. He recounted some experiences in the profile that had not been mentioned in the interview, but they were functionally similar. That is, those additional experiences mentioned in the profile had the same character and function in Carl's life as the experiences reported in the interviews. This suggests that though the recalled incidents may shift, the meanings are remembered. As one tries to recall what happened, the remembered meaning goes in search of an illustrative incident.

Still another confirmation occurred in the accidental juxtaposition of some interview materials and some comments made in a casual conversation with the participant years later. First, an excerpt from an interview with Jane:

I think one of the major things which brought about a change in my attitudes as far as feminist stuff was concerned was in the spring of 1965. I can almost pinpoint the time. I saw a dress pattern in a magazine. It was a rather lowcut dress. And I didn't think anything specific about it being lowcut. I thought, "Gee, that's really a sharp dress." And I made the dress out of red polyester and so forth, and tried it on.

My husband said, "Oh my God, that dress is awful!" And we were invited to a dinner dance. And I had made this dress, and I intended to wear it. I thought it was kind of neat. And it became a big issue that he wasn't going to go with me if I wore it.

Q: Did you wear it?

No, I don't remember. No, I didn't. I didn't. I remember now, I didn't. Then I took a dish of peas and I threw it down the basement steps. I've never thrown anything before or since in our marriage. This is the one time I did. I was so frustrated. And then I was really frustrated, because I had all that mess of peas to clean up. Naturally I had to clean it up. I remember the feelings of hostility after that. I started having chest pains. It was kind of being in a cage, for heaven's sake.

Five years after she told this story, we spent an evening gossiping about old and new times. As we chatted, the subject of feminism came up. "I'll never forget the time," she said, "when I got so mad I threw the plate of peas down . . ." She paused, grinned, "That's right. I told you about that when you interviewed me." Her own repertoire of memories had spontaneously presented the same incident described in the interview. I couldn't have asked for more.

—2—
CONFRONTATIONS

The best way to understand the moments leading to social involvement is to read the interviews themselves. The interviews (and autobiographies) are the source of my information and contain evidence that confirms my interpretations. Thus, the treatment here begins with an interview rather than interpretive conclusions.

Christi is an articulate white woman who has several graduate degrees and works in a helping profession. For well over ten years, she has been involved in civil rights, feminist and related causes and movements. I asked how she had become involved in these social movements.

She began with the time when a newspaper story made her "angry enough to send a dollar away." This led her to join an activist organization and to begin "noticing injustice." Even though she was already sufficiently attuned to injustice that the newspaper article could get her attention, the event marked a turning point for her. From then on, injustices caught her attention in a new way.

One day, by accident, she drove through a black ghetto and was appalled by conditions there, leading to a heightened consciousness of the situation of blacks. Her feminist consciousness developed out of the problems in her marriage and the discovery that it was not just her fault, but that she (and he) were victims of cultural oppression. These and other vignettes together comprise the moments and steps through which she traveled on the path toward social involvement. This particular interview focuses more on the coming to awareness than the activation experience.

I remember a specific event that occurred nine years ago. I read in the *New York Times* about a case in Iowa in which a set of grandparents was given the right to take a child away from its natural father when the father really wanted the child. The mother had died, and at the time of her death the father was not in a position to take care of the child. He had sent the child to the child's maternal grandparents to live on the farm until he could re-establish his life.

After that he married a woman who taught Sunday school and did all that sort of thing. And the court decided that life was better for the child on the farm, than it was with his natural father. That was a new precedent because the court did not find that there was anything wrong with the father, only that the life-style of the grandparents was more in keeping with what the court personally liked.

The Legal Defense Fund was having a national fund drive to help take this to the United States Supreme Court, and it caught my fancy. It was the first cause that I can recall ever really making me angry enough to send a dollar away. I did send some money, and shortly thereafter I received a solicitation for membership, joined, and stayed inactive but started noticing things. Then when we moved to Tennessee, I was approached by some members immediately after we got there and became active because I was asked to, and the need was obvious.

I started noticing injustice in the little town that we moved to shortly after the newspaper incident. I had been very smugly saying that we had integrated schools, that my children were in schools that had blacks and whites. But then one day I had occasion to drive through the section of town where the black children lived, and it was a real slum. The houses were falling down. There were several families in each building; there should have been no families in any of those buildings. It had all been very conveniently out of my sight before. I don't know whether I'd ever driven through and not noticed it before, or whether this was the first time I had driven through it, but it really tugged at my heart.

Q: Did you grow up with a concern for integration, for racial equality, and things of that sort?

I don't think I ever saw a black person until I was in high school. I may have seen them walking in the streets. There were none in the town I grew up in. We also had no Jews. I think I grew up knowing that everybody needs an equal shake, the Christian dogma, but I never really saw it put into action in racial or religious terms. We had a great many wayfarers staying at our home from time to time. My parents were always taking people in—war orphans, people trying to kick narcotic habits, parolees who had no other place to go, children whose parents were in Europe writing books, and just all sorts of people. There was a steady stream of them, and so I know something about the Christian form of giving, the kind that hurts. You know, it's easy to send checks off, but it's not so easy to have someone else at your dinner table. But none of them were black. None of them were of any other race.

It's not a very hard transition to translate what I saw my parents doing and forcing us to do (which I resented as a child) into the obvious. When I saw other people who needed help, then it was a natural thing to try to better the situation too. Only I didn't do it on a one-to-one basis. I tried to make the circumstances better, so that those people wouldn't be in that kind of need. It's because of the way my mother lived her life in my presence when I was a child that I could easily become conscious of suffering on the part of others. She was aware of suffering, and she did what she could to alleviate it on a one-to-one basis. And she used all the family facilities to do that with. We had to share our rooms. There was never any question about it. We were not asked whether we wanted to share our rooms. She informed us that we would have a new roommate— that sort of thing. I remember two of them in particular.

One was a baby named Hugh. He couldn't have been more than ten months old at the time, and we used to watch him eat. We had mashed potatoes a lot, and he would eat three great big bowls full of mashed potatoes every night. Then we all gathered

around the bathtub to watch Mother give him his bath because
he had the most enormous belly, and we changed his name from
Hugh to Huge, naturally, as children will. We enjoyed having
him there. That was great fun because we just thought that he
must never have had anything to eat before he came to our
house, which I'm certain is not true.

And the other one was Mantrap Johnny. I don't remember his
last name. He used to set traps to catch people. I mean nooses
that you'd step into and then the branch would go up and that
sort of thing. He had a knife that he used to put nicks in the
pedestal under the dining room table whenever he caught
somebody. He had a really creative mind. Anyhow, he stayed
with us. He had been in an orphanage, and they couldn't handle
him, so they asked Mother to take him for just a little while to
give them a rest; it lasted for quite some time until Father asked
him to go back. I was the same age as Johnny was at the time.

I think that even though I resented it, I couldn't shake off the
notion that suffering hurts and that I'm in a position to alleviate
it sometimes. I have seen suffering, and just because I would
prefer not to be bothered by it, that doesn't take away my
responsibilities. It doesn't take away my consciousness. I can't
just say, "Well to hell with suffering, I've done my share." Of
course we all say that to some extent because we say no
sometimes.

Q: How is it that you can get inside that person's experience
and someone else looks upon them as a kind of object, like
they'd look at an old car or a flat tire?

I suspect that's a defense mechanism other people have
successfully set up to avoid having to do anything. I don't know.
Not too long ago we had occasion to be in the infirmary of a
convent, where many old nuns are just lying there waiting to die.
I had the children with me. And my oldest daughter was
repulsed when she saw this one woman lying there just groaning.
There was no color in her skin. She was skin and bones. It was a
frightening sight. My daughter was angry with me for having
subjected her to that, and angry with the woman for having the
gall to upset her that way. I was dumb-founded. I really didn't
know how to deal with that because I could not emphathize.

Q: The drive through the community and the reading of the newspaper article both impressed you. Would you get back inside one of those experiences and then retalk it with me? Can you tell me what the street looked like, and who, if anybody, was with you in the car?

It's important. The children were with me. I was feeling my role as mother, guide, educator—all of that and I was feeling very sick. It was an awfully negative thing. I was looking for an address. It happened that it was the same street as we lived on, but everybody knows that there's this end of the street and that end of the same street, and the numbers are the same. There isn't a west and an east, but just everybody knows—only I didn't know.

Something had been delivered to our house, and I was driving down to the other end. We were on our way to buy some fresh fruit and I thought, "We will go down this street and deliver this thing that had been misdelivered to our house." I remember there was a house on the corner that was a really sick green. It was wood frame, two stories; one of the walls didn't meet at the corner. It leaned at about the beginning of the second story, but I think a person could've walked in where the two sides of the house didn't meet.

I saw children running up and down on the wood fire escape and my first thought was, "That whole thing is going to fall down, and they'll all be killed." Then I noticed that all the buildings were about like that. Some of them had torn paper roofs. They were close together. It was a typical small-town slum, but I just had not seen one before.

The street itself was in very poor condition. I had to watch out for chuck holes, whereas the street in front of my house was in good shape. There was a little store there, and I saw kids coming out of the store with candy and junk food, and it all just seemed so sad. I recall the children saying how horrible it was and we should drive fast and get through because it was unpleasant. And I thought it was important to drive slow and see it all, and know that this is what we're doing.

This brings to mind something else—free association. It was at about that time and I think possibly shortly after that and possibly because of that, that we made a commitment to a

Christian Children's Fund foster child—an American Indian. We chose an American Indian because I felt that the damage that we affluent capitalists have done to people all over the world began here and we've got to straighten this one up before we can go abroad. So it was important to me to get an American Indian. We made it a family project. We gave up our Friday night dessert and contributed what would have gone to pay for that to support her. I recall making clothing for her, and doll clothing, and so forth. When I made a dress for her, I would make a dress for the rag doll—to match it. We made a big deal out of it. And I think that all comes from the same sense of things, so it was growing at the time. I think I enjoyed feeling very noble about it, too, of course.

Q: I don't quite understand the connection between the slum children and the foster child.

Well, it has to do with being able to hide poor people on the other side of the tracks or wherever, so that they are out of our vision. And we don't have to contend with our consciences. This is what our way of life, our thinking, our selfishness, doesn't see.

Q: How did you begin to identify as a feminist?

Okay, that was a very personal thing. It had nothing to do with other people suffering; it was my own suffering. My own life was not in good shape and I couldn't identify the reasons why. I was really unhappy, and I had everything that I had always been taught—by society at large, women's magazines, and so forth—is what it takes to make you happy, all the things we strive for. I had a college education, children, and a husband who was good to me and earned lots of money. We had two cars and a big house on the hill. And that didn't hack it—that wasn't nearly enough to make me happy.

For the longest time I assumed being unhappy was my failure. If I have everything it takes to be happy and I'm still not happy, then the fault lies within me. I was introduced to *The Feminine Mystique* by a friend. I read it, saw myself in it, and it lit my fire. I realized from reading that book that not only am I not at fault for not being happy, but neither are any of the other women who

are unhappy and trying to pretend that they're happy. It's not their fault and we need, at first at least, to realize that we are not alone. We've all been fighting it individually, and it seemed like it had to be a movement thing. I could handle my own problems much better, knowing that they were universal problems and that they were not a sign of my failure.

Q: Tell me some more about how that got started.

I attribute it in part, although I wouldn't have at the time, to the move to Tennessee. My own personhood was beginning to emerge, and had to be submerged for that to take place. I think I was on the verge of going to graduate school or getting involved in social action. It was brewing—it was ready to be born, to mix the metaphors. And I felt that that was being taken from me, grasped from me, for my husband's professional betterment. I couldn't articulate that at the time. I just knew that it was very, very painful.

I knew that I didn't matter—that was implicated in the whole decision-making process. If I was going to become suicidal over the move, very well, that was a heavy price to pay, but the road ahead was clear. One can hardly be of less value than that. It took a long time for me to be able to sort through and articulate that. I didn't realize that my personhood was emerging at the time. I look back and see the signs of it and realize that that's where it was beginning. Had my attitude toward the move been a little more realistic, it maybe wouldn't have had to be submerged.

I was very frightened about Tennessee in general—I'd never lived in that part of the country. I knew that's where they had killed Martin Luther King, shot at blacks and anybody who stands up for them. I really didn't know anything else about Tennessee and that was not a realistic assumption of what it was I was getting into. But given my perception of what I was getting into, which I had articulated clearly, and that there was still no question about whether we would move, it necessitated submergence of my person. At the same, it required a positive move on my part to make the children be able to live through the transition positively, so that it was doubly hectic.

I had encouraged them to look favorably on the move, which must have been superhuman. I think that must have been my greatest achievement and no one notices that at all, because I don't have anything on the wall that says that I did do that. I know that I felt that was my job.

The offer to move came out of the blue. I think my husband became tunnel-visioned. Either that, or I never said, "Hey, wait a minute!" Maybe it was a combination. I know it wasn't malicious. After we'd been in Tennessee for two to three years, he told me that he remembered hearing all the things I had said. He remembered my suicide threat, which was no joke. He remembered it all. And he put it in his internal computer and came out with a value of zero on everything that I had said, leaving the decision clear.

I tried to commit suicide. On the way down, I tried to jump out of the car when we hit the Tennessee border. I had told him I was going to and I did. I couldn't get the door open, but we struggled, and there was a cliff, right there. We came in on the old highway. I had every intention of him losing me. And I made that as clear as I could. When I saw the sign that said Welcome to Tennessee, I just couldn't go into Tennessee, and the only way to avoid it was to get out of the car. But I had told him at home—I will commit suicide before I go to Tenessee, I will *not* go to Tennessee, I cannot go to Tennessee. So he was confronted with that— whether he believed it or not is something else. But I wasn't kidding.

My fourth baby was born that year. And I was still impressing people with how much I was accomplishing. People were saying, "I don't know how you do it." So of course, I nursed her so that people would say it even more. I was supermom, absolutely supermom. I got great joy out of having people know that I was being a good mother, and having the evidence for people to know that my kids were the first ones in the block to read, talk, walk, get teeth, whatever it is that kids do. That matters to young mothers.

I recall an incident that I remember gloating about 'cause it was such fun, and it was really a vicious thing to have done. We lived in a small apartment back in New Hampshire, the five of us, and I was keeping my sister's baby for a while. My husband would come in, turn on our very old TV, then go to the kitchen and get a beer and come back and sit down. By the time he had sat down, the TV would be warmed up so that there would be a picture on it. The living room was the only room there was in the house, really. There were the two tiny bedrooms and a little bitty kitchen that we had to eat in. The living room was the central room. You had to go through it to get to any other room. That damn TV was on constantly, and I felt he was watching reruns of junk and not really seeing them. And I resented it very much because it became the master of the house. Nothing else could happen. The kids couldn't read a book; they couldn't do a puzzle; I couldn't talk; I couldn't think; the telephone couldn't be used; nothing could happen while the TV was on. I began to see it as the end of me. So one day I unplugged it and cut off the plug, and flushed it, and didn't say anything.

He came in that night and turned it on, went and got his beer, and sat down. It must have been ten minutes before he realized it wasn't on yet, and he said, "Hmm, TV doesn't seem to be working." I said, "Oh?" and I went on preparing dinner. He fiddled with the knobs and did all the things that men do, kicked it and things like that, to make it work. Nothing happened. Finally he picked up the plug. He said, "Hmm, the plug has been cut off." I said, "Oh?" He said, "Hmm, I wonder how that happened?" I said, "Think a minute." Then he said, "Did you do that?" I said, "Yes," and he said, "Well, why?" I said, "Because that's the only way I know of to keep it off." He said, "That's a really good idea. I've been watching too much TV, lately." So we left it that way for a week, and then he went and bought a new plug. The same thing started happening all over again. We hadn't made any headway at all.

But I felt as if I had won a battle. The TV had become an enemy, and I won a battle. I lost the war, but I won that one battle and it gave me great satisfaction—much too much. I should've turned it off, stood in front of it and said, "Now we're gonna talk!," but I didn't do that. I was still working with women's wiles, you know, different underhanded ways of trying to get my way. It was a delicious victory, though.

My meaning then had to do with being a supermom. And I found that satisfying. I was working toward my degree, and I could see that it was close. I had no idea what I was going to do with it, but it was important to me to get because I had worked for twelve years to get it, you know, off and on—lost credits with transferring, due to his profession. And it was finally in sight. That was exciting to me. After he went to work for a company, we bought a house, and that was a happy year.

I was in a house that I had chosen. It was the kind of house that I thought was a family house. It was an old two-story house with nooks and crannies and glass doorknobs and woodwork and all of that. The children were at a good age. We had two cars finally, so I was free to take the kids to run in the country, or whatever we liked. We had a next-door neighbor who was my children's guardian angel or godfairy or something. She was an artist, and she encouraged the children through painting and so forth. We had plenty of room. The children were happy there. It was just a good Norman Rockwell sort of life—the kind that can't last. It was at the end of the year that we spent in that house that the move to Tennessee came, which crashed everything. First time in our lives we had enough money; there we really had enough money.

So then we moved to Tennessee and meaning changed considerably. There wasn't any meaning for quite a while after we moved to Tennessee. I was close to catatonic; I sat and stared at the wall for months. It was a fancy home, not my kind of home at all. It was the kind of elegant—where you show every nickel you've spent—a chandelier over the dining room table, that, to my mind, only casts shadows when you are trying to read. To other people's minds, it was a beautiful, expensive thing. So I turned the den of our home into pretend New Hampshire. This was my defense mechanism. That den was not in Tennessee. There were no things on the walls, except things the children had painted or drawn. Nothing that we bought in Tennessee was in that room. I don't think that it was as conscious and precise as I make it out now. It was a kind of hiding place from the world. The rest of the house had all the elegancies of the house in it and things that we'd had to buy for the house.

I recall on the day we moved in, the Realtor took a Polaroid picture of the family standing in front of the house and it irked the hell out of me. I did not want my picture to be taken in Tennessee. I wasn't ready yet to face the fact that I was in Tennessee, and that photo sort of immortalized the situation. It cast it. That was the only picture that was taken of me in Tennessee until four or five years later.

We had bought our movie camera the year before, and had been enjoying it. We just didn't even take any more pictures in Tennessee. I couldn't bear to have any pictures taken in Tennessee, so I used that den to escape for a long, long time—much too long. There wasn't any meaning there. There really wasn't any meaning while I was working on my master's degree, either, but I became so busy that it didn't matter. I didn't have a chance to stop and think "What's it all about?" The social activism thing gained momentum as I was doing the master's degree. That took on meaning, but it had nothing to do with family or profession. It was the other part that gradually took over 100 percent of the meaning.

As one digs around in Christi's remarks (with the help of other interviews in which similar patterns are visible), one finds more clues about the nature of moral consciousness. Christi begins by talking about the check she sent off to a good cause (a rather inauspicious beginning). In what sense is "sending a check" a social action or social involvement?

"Acts that are first" stand in two orders of significance in the interviews. One has to do with the structure of the interview itself, while the other has to do with the development of the activist (chapter 5). It is not unusual for first acts to sound either trivial or strange. Pat's first act was to get a kindergarten class started for her son. Al's first act was to teach a Sunday school class on social issues. Neither of these acts seems like much of a beginning for political activism.

The structure of an autobiographical interview requires certain first acts—whatever they may happen to be. The speaker spontaneously crafts a specific story from out of all the complex materials of the past. Some things must be selected, others rejected. The story has to have a beginning and an ending. Requiring a set of firsts, the storyteller selects a beginning that makes sense in light of the thematic unity of the tale. First acts take on meaning in the light of later acts. Al quickly became involved in civil rights marches. Christi went on to over a decade of advocacy activities. Pat was elected to public office.

Having described her first act, Christi moved to a discussion of her parents and socialization experiences. (I chose not to focus the interviews on socialization processes, but readily recorded them when they came up.) Two persons with similar socialization may move in opposite directions in the course of a lifetime. What then is the role that ongoing experience plays in shaping what socialization has already laid down?

Christi was raised with a value system in which concern for the other was emphasized. Good values are essential. The role of further experience in creating changes of perception, interpretation, or feeling sympathetic about what is going on in the world is equally crucial. It is interesting that many of those who have chosen to make long-term studies of the moral life, such as Lawrence Kohlberg and Jean Piaget, cite some experiential incident that got them started on the road toward their research.

Late in life, Louis Raths recounted an amusing incident that may have laid the foundation for his origination of values clarification. When he was in the second grade, he used to suck his sleeve. No amount of Thou-shalt-not or peer ridicule stopped him. Then one day a teacher innocently inquired whether sucking his sleeve was his favorite position. "Some time during the next week or two I stopped doing it," he wrote. His teacher's "nonjudgmental comment stimulated me, I believe, to examine my practice. And I myself rejected it."[1] That sort of approach became a cornerstone of values clarification that Raths would go on to articulate.

There are moments of existential breakthrough that change a person's moral orientation, and moments in which some concern or value in the background of one's life becomes thrust into the foreground of awareness. In a sense, morality becomes real in these experiences—for a latent morality without extension to active sociality is in some respects dead.

The difference between seeing and not seeing is one of the most fundamentally important elements of experience—in this case, moral experience. In other words, the way a person perceives a certain phenomenon establishes the meaning the phenomenon has for that person. An artist or art historian who looks at a painting sees many things that I don't see. Two people who look at the same event see different things, and interpret them differently. Two people driving down the road pass by a slum. One breezes by, thinking about a happy hour; the other imagines himself living inside dilapidated buildings, and is moved to reflect on the meaning of poverty in the midst of affluence. Two people turn on the radio and hear Paul Harvey. One says, "Oh, only him," and turns the dial; the other listens with interest. Or, perhaps both listen. One spends the time thinking of the gaps in the commentator's logic, while the other thinks it all makes great sense. The framework of interpretation that a person brings to bear on daily life experiences is foundational to the way that person experiences reality. Thus, a moral framework—perceiving the world in moral terms—is prior to, and foundational for, moral reflection, decision, and action.

What is it, then, that Christi began to see? She saw black children playing in dangerous slum housing. Children clearly have been a major part of her life and concern. Her parents took in children; she sent off a check because a child's well-being was at stake; she saw children in the slum; and she put a lot of energy into her own children. Slum children touched her in a way that perhaps something else might not have.

The slum "tugged at her heart." In her second telling of the slum incident, she went into greater detail. She recalled that the slum was at the other end of her own street. "I had to watch out for chuck holes, whereas the street in front of my house was in good shape." The condition of the street took on more meaning because it was same street on which she lived. Comparison between one's own situation and that of others not only triggers awareness, it gives shape to moral judgment.

Finally, she was asked about her feminist identity. "That was a very personal thing. It had nothing to do with other people suffering. It was my own suffering." *The Feminine Mystique* "lit my fire," leading her to reinterpret her own situation in moral terms. Before her reinterpretation, certain things had been perceived as her personal failures—and thus her fault—afterwards she would perceive that the whole system of cultural oppression was the source of, and thus blameworthy for, her situation. The whole locus and weight of responsibility shifted. It was not her fault!

The Variety of Experiences

The experiences in the interviews that most typically led to increased awareness were: (1) being discriminated against, (2) witnessing the suffering of some other person, (3) bonding with someone or gaining access to the meaning of their life-world, and (4) confrontation with discontinuities in oneself.

1. The experience of discrimination: James Forman titled his autobiography *The Making of Black Revolutionaries*. What is it that creates revolutionaries?—experiences like the one with which he began his book.

He had just left the University of Southern California library. After five hours of studying for an exam, he was enjoying the stars and the night air. "Hey boy! You there! Come here!" a policeman called out from his car. "There's been this robbery and you look like the one who did it," he said. The police made Forman get into their car, took him to the station, and beat him.[2]

The experience, which hit him suddenly, was an interruption of normal patterns and routines. He felt that it was undeserved—not just random unfairness, but rampant racism. The experience was intensely personal; it touched him emotionally and physically.

Other persons who have been discriminated against report long-term suffering without quite being able to identify it as originating in discrimination. Typically, they speak of a series of cumulative occasions, the weight of which finally breaks through on one sharply experienced occasion, enabling them to reperceive their situation as preventable discrimination—someone else's fault.

2. The experience of seeing other people suffer: Russian revolutionary Angelica Balabanoff mused, "Whenever I am asked how I came to turn my back upon my family, upon the comfort and luxury of my home in southern Russia and to become a revolutionist, I am at a loss for an answer." Yet she remembered, "Once when I saw some peasants on our estate kiss the border of my father's coat when he returned from a long journey, I cringed with shame." Early in life she first met poverty when she went with her mother to the local house

where the poor and insane were crowded together. "My first realization of inequality and injustice grew out of these experiences in my early childhood."[3]

One of the research participants, Thomas, recalls a series of events in which he saw other people suffer, and then recounts how he had been threatened. Thomas is a full-time social service worker and activist.

When I started college I was an ultraconservative fundamentalist. I didn't drink, smoke, play cards. I hadn't had a beer or been to the movie by the time I graduated from college. [Then he moved to the big city.] **And the influence of the city was just heavy, heavy, heavy. You couldn't walk out your front door without confronting it. I remember the first time I walked out of my front door and saw four cops beating the ——— out of a black man in my front yard, just beating the crap out of him. I looked at him and there was nothing I could do but get the hell out of there. And then for months later you ask yourself, "What could I have done? What can I do? I guess what I can do is to get involved in something that's going on in this community—to deal with oppressive policemen."**

I worked for four years as a surgical tech in the emergency room of the county hospital. In that zoo you constantly feel the pain, because you're dealing with people who are victims of pain all the time—rat bites, disease and gunshots, knifings, beatings, car wrecks, and so forth. That was an important part of my life.

[Thomas spent time on skid row, drank wine with winos, and worked with two different youth gangs.] **I got to feel the pain of the oppressed that way. I don't believe there ever was a click experience. I didn't even know it was happening when it was happening. It wasn't a planned kind of thing at all. It's only in reflecting afterward that I learned from it. It was probably the most important part of my education.**

I was running with a nun who was Daniel Berrigan's housekeeper, working with the Weathermen, and organizing the Socialists. We organized the Washington April moratorium. We organized a picket line around a plant and caused the company to spend millions of dollars putting in new anti-pollution filters.

One night our office nearly burned to the ground. And there were Molotov cocktails found on what was left of the roof. We

figured it was the narcotics agents. About two weeks later my car was gunned by an automatic weapon. I had just gotten out of it and walked into the house, and I heard bam, bam, bam, bam. I came out and the whole side of my car was full of bullet holes. I immediately went back into my house and packed my suitcase. Some of my friends came over and we worked through it for hours, and I decided not to leave.

Even though Thomas' awareness was generated by the suffering of people other than himself, the experiences were, in some respects, quite similar to those of James Forman. He witnessed suffering first hand. He was personally drawn into physical and emotional suffering. The suffering of other people was intense, provoking deep feelings in him. He took their suffering upon himself—it became his.

3. Experiences that bond people together: The most familiar example of this sort of experience is the sense of we-ness, arising when people are drawn together by a common disaster. (For example, when a community unites to save a child who has fallen into a well, the community may focus for days on getting the child out alive. In the meantime, everyone develops a we-spirit.)

The next interview excerpt describes bonding. Ben is now a full-time community organizer. One incident he recalls occurred during his college days and was rooted in his growing affection for the Appalachian children he worked with. Over a period of time he gained more access to their life-world. The children became fully real to him. He found himself bonding with elements of their shared humanity, and his commitment to social action grew out of this event and others like it.

We had this program for Appalachian children. Every Saturday we'd drive a van and pick up the children and bring them to the college. It was mostly recreation, tutorial stuff, making friends with the kids or whatever. Well, I really got into that. I really liked those children. And I became close to a few families. I was even invited over one night for coon.

They had eight children—lived up in the hills. The father had been a coal miner in shaft mines. The strip mine laid him off. They had been on welfare for a lot of years. They had at one time thirteen children, but five were killed in a fire. So that working with that kind of children, talking with them, and playing with them made a big impact.

I once had to walk up to their school to make an announcement about a picnic. Some of the kids were outside for gym class. And they just started screaming and shouting, and all gathered around me. And kids started to shout high out the windows in the school, "There's Ben. There's Ben." It was real neat. I really got close to a lot of people from a poverty setting.

One of the things that moved me was that they had to be so mature to survive. Little boys could hunt. The eleven-year-old boys were making out and stealing. They stole me an orange one day [laughs] from the store. They stole them one, so they stole me one too. We just developed close rapport with them where they'd share these kind of things.

We'd get angry at them. One day a little boy took off, decided he was mad at us for some reason, and he just took off. He was going home. And he just took off running through the woods. I took off after him, chased him for a long time. Finally I caught him. I just grabbed him and held him. We just sat there and held each other, and I cried over this kid many nights. At the same time in class, we were reading Bultmann and Bonhoeffer.

Part of the experience was tied up with seeing the ongoing suffering and deprivation to which the Appalachians were subject. But the dominant motif is the bond Ben developed with them, especially the children. He was able to get inside the meaning of their daily life experience. He came to identify with them, to see them as real human beings who laughed, cried, struggled, and celebrated. He liked them. His theological readings helped create an interpretive framework that was consistent with his daily experience.

Some bonding experiences are of the "I really identified with" sort, while others are of the "I really liked," or "I came to appreciate" sort. It was possible to identify with someone in a novel or something seen on television—"I really identified with the students who were shot at Kent State." Appreciative bonding more typically grew out of close acquaintance with the meaning-world of the other person.

4. Confrontation with oneself: The interview quoted below is rather unusual among the experiences gathered. Joe reported that his biggest awakening occurred as he was driving alone down an expressway.

The experience that was probably the most crucial in a personal change was the one that happened at the time of Martin Luther King's death. I was at the University of Maryland. And, about halfway through the morning, some disturbances began to break out in some of the high schools in the city. So partially out of sympathy and partially out of the fear of the disturbances coming onto the campus, they called off classes.

It was about mid-morning, about 10:30, that I was driving back to my home. I had the radio on because I was listening to the newscast. I remember very clearly driving down a street toward my home. I had taken some roads that would keep me away from the high school areas where they were having problems. I was listening to the radio to the people who were talking about what was going on. They had a news crew in a helicopter circling around the area where there were some disturbances going on.

The students had gotten together and had left the high school, and were crossing one of the major freeways running through Baltimore. And of course there was a lot of fear that the group was going to riot the downtown area, break out windows—that kind of thing. I remember listening to all of this, and the announcer said something to the effect that there were two helicopters circling the area—that he and his news crew were in one and that in the other helicopter, the police chief and some policemen were circling the area.

I was visualizing the whole thing. In my mind's eye I saw these black students running across and blocking off the highway and kind of a mass of them coming down through the downtown area. And then for some reason or other, I found myself thinking about a picture I'd seen in *Life* magazine a few weeks before, where they had one of those assault helicopters that they were using in Nam at the time. They had big old machine guns on the side of those things, and they would open them up, and they would rake the area. And I found myself thinking—you know I wish they had one of those helicopters there so they could just mow those people down as they came across the highway. I was

really kind of visualizing that whole process going on in my head as I drove home.

Then all of a sudden [snaps his finger] I stopped that, and I said, "What is this? I mean, does that fit into who I really am? I mean, do I really feel that way? Do I really believe that way? Is that the way I really want things to be?" I had a very strong kind of church background that made me concerned from a religious-moral point of view. I said "No!" And all of a sudden I realized that I was part of that problem, that I'd grown up in a suburb, that I was full of fear and hate, and had no understanding or conception of what anybody else was really experiencing.

I spent a lot of time listening to media reports—they had black people, spokesmen for the city, and so forth constantly on trying to keep the riot situation cool. And all of a sudden, out of that kind of experience, I decided that something needed to be done.

The riots stirred up his fears, broke the complacency of his awareness. He was wounded by the rubbing together of jagged incongruities in his own consciousness. Part of his inner dialogue was a conversation between parts of himself. "Does that fit into who I really am? Do I really feel that way? Do I really believe that way? Is that the way I really want things to be? I said, 'No!' " He juxtaposes one set of feelings and thoughts with another, trying to arrive at one congruent frame of interpretation out of these discordant realities. He inquires not only into his own values and vision, but his own moral identity—"Does that fit who I really am?"

—3—
COMING
TO AWARENESS

Metaphors like "It was an eye-opener" and "It really hit me" are used typically to describe the coming-to-awareness experience. They provide clues to the way consciousness experiences events. "It was an eye-opener" is experienced as an enlightenment; "It really hit me" is experienced as a body blow.

A metaphor is a word or phrase that takes a literal meaning from one context, and uses it to add dimension or connotation to the meaning of another context. Thus, "It dawned on me" uses the word "dawned" to add extra imagery to the experience of discovery. Metaphors can lose their metaphorical quality by being overused. "I saw what she meant" is such a common expression that it no longer carries much additional imagery; the surplus of meaning disappears. However, if the person speaks the same metaphor with great drama and emotion, its metaphorical qualities are reconstituted—it has a new liveliness. The participants in this research project tended to see the world in rather dramatic terms and expressed themselves with a certain intensity. Those who read the interviews will have to use their imagination to provide the imagery and drama originally there, but lost when the spoken lifescript was reduced to typescript.

Some philosophers believe that metaphors are merely expressions of emotion, low on meaning, and therefore unworthy of scholarly investigation. The study of metaphors has recently undergone a renaissance. Paul Ricoeur suggests that metaphors communicate not a dearth, but a surplus of meaning. Hannah Arendt writes that metaphors are at the very heart of poetry. All abstract thought, including metaphysics, she suggests is finally based on metaphor. H. Richard Niebuhr pointed out some years ago that even such a hard-core empiricist as John Locke was dependent on metaphors to communicate his ideas.[1]

Those philosophical treatments that have focused on metaphors have taken literary metaphors, especially poetic rather than interview-type, as paradigms of the genre. Though "the poetic image is a sudden salience on the surface of psyche,"[2] the poet has plenty of chances to rework the metaphor and its context before sending a draft off to the publisher. The person being interviewed has but an unselfconscious millisecond gap between thought and vocalization—the metaphor is only poetry aborning. Interview metaphors are more spontaneous and intuitive than crafted.

The metaphor, as part of the informative or presentive aspect of the tale, is a means by which the speaker attempts to transcend the limits of mundane speech—tries to paint a picture, rather than draw a diagram, or makes the description more dramatic by invoking expressive and imaginative imagery. The speaker tries to re-present some of the excitement and emotional meaning of past experiences by giving them fresh existential qualities. Meaningful events from the past thus come alive.

Even at the level of daily chitchat, metaphors reveal images that are lively to a person. When I took up sailing, nautical metaphors crept into casual conversations and classroom lectures. When large groups of people believe a metaphor is apt, it becomes a part of common discourse. In the 1960s the submarine *Thresher* sank to the bottom of the ocean and was crushed. A naval officer of my acquaintance tried to introduce the metaphor "thresher," meaning a crushing experience—as in "It was a thresher"—into public conversation. Apparently he hoped that the ship's crew would be memorialized by the metaphor being taken into the everyday language of our culture. The effort was unsuccessful, but illustrates something of the connection between metaphor and shared meaning in a culture. The examination of metaphors not only reveals things about the person who uses them, but taps into cultural meanings that are preserved and transmitted in language. The basis for my interpretation can only be the interviews, but participants' persistent use of culturally common metaphors suggests that these experiences are shared rather widely.

Five clusters of metaphor rooted in people's experience of their own bodies are found in the interviews. Consciousness likens itself to body-based experiences—persons describe experiences in terms of what is most lively to the consciousness, namely the body.

Consciousness is housed in, or framed by, one's body. The interplay between body and consciousness is reflexive. The closer something comes to one's body, the greater the effect on one's consciousness. When the policeman grabbed James Forman, the impact doubled. Emotionally compelling events affect one's consciousness, precisely because the emotions are so much a part or expression of one's body.

Many phenomenologists explore the relationships of body, experience, and consciousness.[3] They distinguish between the lived-body and the body as studied by science. The former is the body as subjectively experienced; the latter, the body as physical object among other physical objects. The lived-body is a primary boundary and medium through which the world is experienced. It makes a great deal of difference whether one is three feet seven or seven feet three, whether one is black or white, whether one is male or female. Maulana Ron Karenga went so far as to say "The fact that I am Black is my ultimate reality."[4] The character of one's embodiment is one of the most fundamental realities we experience.

Stewart and Mickunas summarize some aspects of the lived-body receiving the special attention of phenomenologists.[5] The lived-body is a center of orientation. Our bodies are the center points for organizing our perceptions of time and space. We locate up and down, here and there, even in some sense, now and then by the positionality of our bodies at a given moment. Time is measured by the deepening of the wrinkles on our brow. Our bodies are not only the center of our perceptual orientation, but also "in the broader sense of the center of active orientation."[6]

The lived-body is a source of motives. The needs for bodily survival become major shapers of the ways of our days—our bodies are the locus of, as we call it, gut feelings. The Hebrew root for "compassion" is a feeling from "the womb." Love is experienced as an outpouring of the heart—one's skin crawls in fear; anger is burning fire radiating from the torso. These emotions push us toward social acts somewhat as biological drives push us toward physical survival.

The lived-body is the organ of action. It is through our bodies that our consciousness is related to the world—both receptively and actively. The body is a mediator between consciousness and the outer world. It is through our bodies that we gear into the activities of the world. The motions of our minds are translated into movements of hands and feet. The ways in which we are active or passive and the ensuing results are experienced and stored in our body's memory.

The lived-body is also the way we become aware of other people and in turn present ourselves to them. Perceptions of difference in age, handicap, race, gender, even wealth and culture, provide a certain structuring of human social interaction. It is difficult to forget one is talking to a person of a different race, gender, or class.

It is surprising, given the importance of one's lived-body to experience in general, that ethicists have devoted so little attention to this. The most significant work has been by feminist theologians—perhaps because women are more sensitive to the presence and rhythms of their bodies than men who have tended to treat their bodies in a utilitarian manner.[7]

The body is a compelling medium through which we become conscious of experiences; it shapes both the possibility and the character of their reception. The interview participants' extensive and emotional use of body metaphors suggests significance beyond simple linguistic references to levels of experiential meaning. The intensity with which body metaphors are uttered suggests the primary, visceral level at which these experiences were received.

It is not surprising to discover that the metaphors that occur most frequently in the interviews to describe awareness-experiences are body-rooted. The experience of one's body becomes a literal base for the transferred (metaphorical) meaning describing consciousness. This can be seen in the five major clusters of metaphors appearing in the interviews.

1. Body-impact metaphors: People use images from their bodily experience to describe by analogy what occurred to their consciousness. "It hit me." "I was shocked." "It made a dent on me." "It grabbed me." "I was crushed." "It blew my mind." "It impressed me." "My gut reaction was that it wasn't fair." "Partly it's evidence that's piled up on you." "It sticks in my head." "It stretched my mind." "I was ready to be born." "That cut me deeply. It was a traumatic experience." "You may intellectually verbalize racial equality, but you don't in your down-deep part feel that way." Corporeal metaphors express a sensation of consciousness which is like the sensations of the body. Thus, "it hit me" might have been stated more fully, "When I had that experience, my mind/feelings were struck in the same manner as when my body was hit on other occasions." And since the experiences affected their emotions (which are so integrally a part of embodiment) their consciousness was stirred up all the more.

2. Kinetic metaphors—the experience of the body in motion: "It was a turning point." "It turned my head around." "It began my searching." "It was a moving experience," or literally "My consciousness was moved by that experience." "I shifted." "We travel little roads." "I made a quantum leap." "It was like she just made the first step, and once I recognized the first step, then [steps] two, three, and four and five became very clear. I recognized that the book hadn't gone far enough." These metaphors liken the passage of one's consciousness through space (and time) to the movement's of one's body. These metaphors are of change and of turning, progression, and traveling. They are also metaphors of reorientation, growth, and kinesis through space.

3. Metaphors of spatiality—the experience of space: These metaphors place more emphasis on the sentient aspects of body experience of space than the kinetic moving-through-space aspects cited above. "You get locked in at a very early age." "It was like being in a cage." "We had found a home, and that home was the National Organization for Women." "I had this

sensation of being trapped." "I was still half-bound in a way." "My father was gone; that was a closed door." "I allowed all that to put me in a corner." "I felt like I was in a white box, a glaring white box." "What a narrow, narrow, narrow world I had lived in. My God, here is the great big world out there."

4. Metaphors of perception, based on the physical act of seeing: "It opened my eyes" is the most common. "It was quite an awakening to discover." "All of a sudden it came like a blinding flash." "I couldn't focalize it in my mind." "It was an illuminating experience." "Suddenly I became aware I had my eyes closed." "I began to hear things and see things I'd never heard and seen before." "It dawned on me."

The Western tradition has emphasized the superiority of sight over the other senses. Metaphors emphasizing hearing were rare. Seeing is believing, by and large. But what really counts is the seeing, the discernment of consciousness. Sight orients our bodies to phenomena in our visual field. Perception, interpretation, and emotion orient our lives to the human realities constituting our moral field.

5. Coming-together metaphors: Some are tactile; others are actional—the body does something. "I began to connect." "I started putting the pieces back together." I pulled together a whole bunch of things." "It took a long time for me to be able to sort through and articulate that." "I had been pulling all this together for two years." "That's when I see it all coming together." Whether it came together by itself, or was pulled together may not be so much the point as that some new whole emerged from previously disparate parts. A few non-body metaphors were used to describe this coming-together experience. "It all jelled." "It was a catalyst." "It crystallized all those things that had been running around in my mind for all those years." "Running around in my mind" is an extended body-based metaphorical phrase. Thus, there are at least five identifiable clusters of metaphors rooted in embodiment, but used to describe acts and states of consciousness rather than acts and states of the physical body.

In order to unravel the implications of these clusters, some categories will have to be reshuffled. While "it came like a blinding flash" is physiologically related to seeing, the experience of a blinding flash is as much an experience of shock as of sight. (It is curious that in our language a *blinding* flash is a flash that makes one *see better*. One is shocked, blinded to an old reality, before being able to see a new one.) Thus, "It came as a blinding flash" belongs as much with "I was shocked," as "It opened my eyes." One has to examine not only the literal referent of the metaphor, but the experience it describes.

Metaphors provide an imaginative means of self-expression. They describe experienced reality fully—dramatically. But the metaphors can be examined at another level. As spontaneous utterances of consciousness, they may provide relatively unfiltered expressions of the way consciousness experiences its own structure and change. Thus, when the speakers use metaphors to describe their change experiences, the metaphors reveal not only their conscious sense of what happened, but aspects of the intentional or constitutive structure of consciousness.[8] At a pre-conscious level, metaphors reveal something about the structure of the consciousness that thrust the metaphor into existence. One can read metaphors not only for what they describe or express, but for what they indicate about consciousness, as well.

Frames of Reference

Coming to awareness is experienced partly as the constitution or reconstitution of a frame of reference. The word frame suggests a shape or pattern that forms or holds something in place. We speak of picture frames, window frames, and the framing of a house. A frame outlines, holds, or arranges certain materials. The original meaning of the word is to profit, to be of use, or to fashion.

My use of "frame" is analogous to Parsons' use of "frame of reference" within a theory of action, or Goffman's *Frame Analysis*.[9] A frame of reference (Parsons) articulates the basic limiting possibilities (assumptions) within which a theory will be shaped. A theory itself is a smaller frame within which facts will be organized. To change one's theory is to change one's frame of reference, in turn changing the meaning and relation of the data.

A frame at the level of experience and consciousness (Goffman) performs much the same function as theories do in the disciplines. A cognitive frame orders information. An affective frame organizes emotional responses. A perceptual frame permits seeing. A frame, then, is something that organizes and makes possible our ways of relating to experienceable reality. Consciousness is a series of more or less well-articulated frames.

Edward Tiryakian points out that the frames of consciousness, which orient us to the world, typically function at an assumptive level—below awareness.

> We perceive what is external to us, including others, in a multi-layered medium of meanings constituting an "assumptive frame of reference," which I shall refer to in abbreviated form as AFR. The AFR is a general orientation to the world within which human subjects act and react toward others, make projects, and evaluate events.[10]

The significance of the AFR for the individual and the society is incalculable. At the societal level the AFR is the ethos of a society.[11] At the individual level, the AFR determines one's orientation to phenomena—whom one listens to or whom one ignores, what constitutes admissible or inadmissible information, and so on. When we watch a clown slip on a banana peel, we frame the event as comedy rather than a painful accident. An emotional AFR establishes one's basic optimism or pessimism, one's hope or fear for the future. As a moral phenomenon, our frames determine our orientation toward people and nature.

Assumptive Frames of Reference are a more important moral ordering than principles, rules, arguments, or evidence. For example, our belief that all races are biologically equal is a moral AFR based on a humanistic assumption. There is really no solid, hard-core, ultimately provable evidence that this is true. But we continue to believe it and should. If someone presents us with IQ test scores showing one race inferior to another, a person with one AFR attacks the testing program, while a person with a different AFR believes that the tests have documented the obvious.

A person's view of homosexuality and lesbianism is more grounded in one's orientation to gays than the pro and con arguments used. One's orientation to a subject leads one to seek out facts that fit, experts who make sense (having already determined what it means to make sense) and conclusions that fit inside the frame of assumptions—at least until the frame itself is successfully challenged.

One's AFR determines whether one focuses the weight of attention on the aborted fetus or on the potential mangling of the lives of both mother and child. Many persons, both intelligent and moral, were strong supporters of American involvement in Vietnam. Brilliant rationality can work inside a frame of reference leading one to present carefully reasoned arguments for war. Frames as preconscious orderings of human reality are foundations of morality. Thus, to change one's frame of reference is to change one's moral world.

One's moral orientation is one's stance toward moral phenomena, which inclines one to relate to events in such a way that convincing rationality and fitting emotions follow (while one claims to pronounce the truth). Arguments and feelings tend to be arranged within a frame of reference that may not be addressed at all by counterarguments, no matter how rational or passionate. This is not to suggest that discourse is to no avail; it is rather to recognize that people with radically different frames of reference have a hard time communicating effectively because the reference points for the conversation are so very different. This recognition suggests the importance of studying frames and their changes.

Assumptive frames of reference are gradually formed in primary and secondary socialization. In an arresting passage Berger and Luckmann suggest:

> The age at which, in one society, it may be deemed proper for a child to be able to drive an automobile may, in another, be the age at which he is expected to have killed his first enemy. An upper-class child may learn the "facts of life" at an age when a lower-class child has mastered the rudiments of abortion technique. Or, an upper-class child may experience his first stirrings of patriotic emotion about the time that his lower-class contemporary first experiences hatred of the police and everything they stand for.[12]

In a separate manuscript my co-authors and I describe the significance of a frame of reference:

A frame of reference is powerful because: (1) it is built out of the sum of the meaningful experiences of our lives—hence it is the cumulative wisdom of our years, our gradually formed perspective on life; (2) it is composed of assumptions, that is, things we don't ordinarily stop to examine—the taken-for-granted things, things that have an of-course-it's-that-way character; and (3) it sets up an orientation toward life, a filter through which we screen what we see, how we interpret it, how we evaluate it, and how we act toward it.[13]

Individual frames of reference are subjective meaning structures of the various parts of our consciousness in relation to the varied fields of everyday activity. Comprehensive frames of reference set our basic orientation to reality as a whole, and as such constitute our basic systems of meaning.

Frames organize our relationship to reality. The manner in which we relate to reality is a moral, esthetic, and theological question. The question of our relationship to social (human) reality is clearly a moral matter; so is our relationship to nature. Even our relationship to the cosmos or ultimate meaning and reality (if seen as separate from our relationship to people and nature) has a moral dimension. Religious traditions show ample evidence of moral wrestling with ultimate reality—from ritual acts of grace and forgiveness to moral codes and conduct.

The notion of "frames" is suggested by metaphors used in the interviews. Five dominant images present themselves. The first two deal with breaking down a previous frame, so that a new one can take its place. These images are "triggering" and "tipping" (the last straw) experiences. Two images describe the constitution of a frame—the "coming together," and the "getting it in focus" experience. A fifth image emerges from "flash of light"—"it dawned on me" metaphors.

1. Frame breaking: triggering events. Two of the older persons interviewed mentioned that *The Autobiography of Lincoln Steffens* had brought them important insight about the nature of evil in human association.[14] Steffens, a turn-of-the-century muckraking journalist, uses the same sort of dramatic imagery that appears in the interviews. At one point he describes his own thickheadedness—how stubbornly his consciousness holds on to an old frame of reference, and how difficult it is to make a breakthrough.

I seem to have had a conception, a diagram, of life which every new discovery wrecked or, if it held, had no place for new facts. Facts. It seems to me now that facts have had to beat their way into my head, banging on my brain like the bullets from a machine gun to get in; and it was only by being hit over and over again that I could let my old ideal and college-made picture of life be blown up and let the new, truer picture be blown in. No wonder some men cannot learn; they are subject only to a few shots, not riddled with volleys, daily, all their lives.[15]

Many of the body-impact metaphors suggest the manner in which a major change of consciousness occurs. "It hit me." "I was shocked." "It blew my mind." Other non-body metaphors have a similar import, such as, "It was the triggering incident." Because some frames are firmly fixed in consciousness, it may take a shock to break them open.

A triggering event may be sharp, sudden, and dramatic. A previous frame of consciousness has to be penetrated or shattered in order to make way for the eventual reconstitution of a new frame: "It confronted me and everything started coming down."

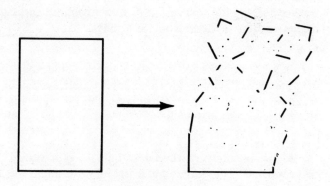

Figure One

Confrontation sometimes creates breakthroughs, interrupting the taken-for-granted routines of daily life.

The jolt of the uncommon, emerging in the midst of the common, awakens that in you of which until now you were not aware, and by so doing effects a subtle shift in you and a change in the world itself. You now see it, for the first time, really.[16]

The experience that occasions a sudden change of awareness commands attention. There are, of course, degrees of drama. The underlying precipitant seems to be a jarring or disruption of a frame, occasioned by some incongruity. Said Wanda, a white female:

One thing does stick out in my mind. I was taking an advanced course in political science. The professor suggested we see a politically oriented movie at a local theater and then come back and discuss it.

There were very few of us in the class. One black woman was working on her master's degree, and she brought out the fact that she couldn't go to the theater and see the movie. Here she was halfway through a master's degree, but she wasn't allowed to buy a ticket to go in and see this movie to come back and discuss it in class.

I was kind of enraged. No, it was more disbelief that in this country this woman who had brains—she was brilliant, had worked her way through college—and she couldn't go down four blocks and buy a ticket and see a movie.

Bill, a black professional, recounts an occasion when his fear of whites was alleviated. He speaks of it as both a religious and a racial conversion. The army had taken this inner city black to a small western all-white town.

And one morning my wife said, "I am going to church." And there was this little church and it was all white and it was in the middle of Podunk, Nebraska, population about two [laughs]. And she was going. And the kid had just been born. Really I was a little afraid. She said she was going, and I said "Well, okay. I'm going with you, but why don't we lay here a little bit longer." I tried all the usual stops and nothing worked, 'cause she has gotten up and put on the clothes and she was going to go.

And so when she got ready to walk out of the door, I saw I

couldn't stop her, so I was going to go with her. I jumped in, "Hold on," you know—jumped in, put on my clothes and then I went with her to this church. It was all white. It was a little small barn that had been renovated.

And we walked in and I was terrified [laughs]. That was the only way I could describe it. I was terrified, and all these eyes turned around, and we walked in and some of them got big as saucers—talk about black folks' eyes. And I looked, and I said, "Let's sit down here." We sat down in the back of the building. The man preached and preached. All of the time I'm watching all these people watching me; kids looking back every once in a while and saying something to their mammas and fathers. All of a sudden the man finished the sermon, and invitation, communion, what have you, and the dismissal prayer.

And when he had said the dismissal prayer it seemed that everybody in that church turned around and started toward the back. I mean not in the normal sense, but it seemed like they all snapped around and started running to the back. I thought we were gone. I really did [laughs]. I jumped up; I jumped up and said, "That's it, let's go." And left her. I left her and the baby. She was holding the baby, and I was running for the door. Not literally running, but I was quickstepping, let me put it that way. And I was trying to get her to come on, but she was surrounded. But I was going to the door. I could bring back help. And two guys stepped in front of the door. "Oh God, they've got us." And the guy reached out and extended his hand and patted me on the back. I was shocked. I was shocked, and I think that was sort of my religious conversion as far as the church was concerned right that day. The fact that there were whites who were concerned. It was a really big surprise to me.

2. Frame breaking: tipping events. Not all frame breaking events come like a bolt out of the blue. Many times they are experienced more like the last straw, the straw that broke the camel's back. Some people retrospectively spoke of having been "ripe" or "ready" for the change. Then came a tipping event. Incident after incident occurs; event piles on event until a breakthrough occurs.

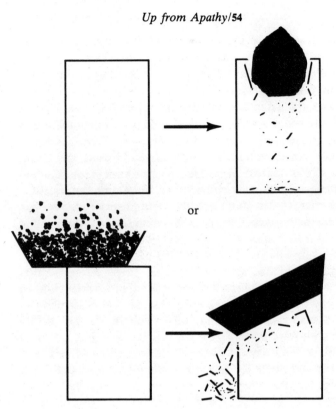

Figure Two

George, a black male, experienced discrimination repeatedly. Then finally one day, it drove him to activism:

I was born in Mississippi in 1920. I went to high school and Tuskegee, and was not an activist at that time because that was in the thirties and no black man was much of an activist in Mississippi.

I moved to New York and became frustrated and angry that I was unable to do like my white classmates at the college and get a job with electricians or engineers or for apprentice work in the summertime. I had to work as a busboy in a hotel or some place like that in order to make money. That made me very conscious of the race problem, but not enough to become an activist.

I became a soldier in World War II. I ended up flying an airplane as an artillery observer. I flew a Piper Cub, and went to artillery officer candidate school. When I finished I didn't get a commission because they were overstaffed with blacks, so I went overseas as a sergeant to Italy. I had to wait in line for one of the lieutenants to get killed. I became very angry about that. I flew half the war as a staff sergeant and wasn't allowed to be the pilot of a fighter plane or bomber or fly over Germany. After the war I studied liberal arts in Italy. This old man introduced me to Marxism and the whole concept of social injustice and social justice. That individual represents a turning point in my thinking, and had more influence on me than anybody else.

I came back to the United States. Atlanta was still segregated. I became very angry about that. But I still had not become an activist. I got married and had two children. I think I became an activist on the day that I moved into Atlanta right down the street from a white elementary school and I had to bus my child across town to a black elementary school. I tried to get my child in the white school and was arrested for doing so. As a result of that I became very active in the NAACP working for school integration, and eventually in job discrimination.

I hadn't been politically oriented, and I wasn't a member of a political party. I had never voted in an election in my life. My anger built up and I became involved in the local chapter of the Congress of Racial Equality. We put out picket lines during the sixties. I went on a freedom ride in Mississippi and spent forty days in jail. Later I became the first black elected to the Board of Education in this century in the city I had moved to.

George's remarks describe the activation experience more than the coming-to-awareness experience. Anger built up until finally it broke through and drove him to do something about racial discrimination. Some of the structural characteristics of awareness and activation are the same, although emotion and content may differ. The awareness experience typically comes as a sense of hurt in response to suffering, whereas activation is more often triggered by anger.

My own data, so far, indicate that each of the men and women in leadership positions in the Gray Panthers comes from either a deeply committed religious background or a family which stressed service to the community, or both, but that these were not enough in themselves to promote political activism. The impetus for activism seemed to be generated through some event or turning point that had a radicalizing effect . . . When [Maggie Kuhn] was told that she would have to retire at the prescribed age, she experienced first shock, she said, then *rage* . . . .[17]

As the frame goes, so goes the picture. In both triggering and tipping events, once the old frame has collapsed, the picture within the frame needs to be reorganized. Sometimes a frame simply collapses without there being any immediate sense of direction about what a new picture might look like. Other times, the moment of penetrating insight creates the breakthrough, thereby suggesting at least the direction, if not the full implication of the picture. Thus, "I started noticing" suggests that the germ of insight was present in the breakthrough. At this point, one doesn't quite know what a new picture will look like, but one is aware that the old one will no longer suffice.

Once an old frame has collapsed, there is a flow of information into the newly created vacuum. "It began my searching." "It started me thinking." Over a period of time, a new frame is fully constituted, taking the place of the old. Old experiences are reinterpreted, and newly occurring experiences are assimilated into the new frame of reference. Gradually the frame thickens with meaning until it becomes firm.

3. The coming together of pieces is a step in the reconstitution of a frame. "Finally I started pulling the pieces back together. It all fit together. It made sense." Lincoln Steffens records the moment when the duty-oriented and conscientious district attorney of St. Louis, Joe Folk, related how he, Folk, had been commanded by the party machine to hire certain people and to look aside when ballot boxes were stuffed.

> When Folk described it thus, with startled eyes, you could see that his picture of the world was being all slashed to pieces.
> "I and my office, the criminal law, was to be run by—criminals!"
> He put it like that. He had imagination. He must have had, because, piecing together the fragments of his torn picture, he startled my imagination and made me a picture, too. I was taking the single, separate facts of political corruption and joining them into a new view of the city as it is.[18]

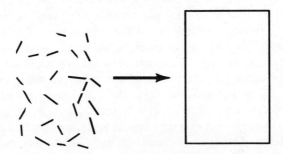

Figure Three

While the coming-together-of-pieces experience is a further implication of a frame-change event, such change also occurs without a frame first having to be broken down. Some persons are not aware of having a prior frame that needs to be broken down—in this sense, they are creating a particular frame for the first time. The pieces might have all been there before, but now for the first time they come together to make a picture. "It was like many threads coming together." "I began to pull together a whole bunch of things." "It all jelled." "That's one of those moments when I see it all coming together." "It's like something on the right side meshed with something on the left. You pull out a plug and the two worlds flow together." "The pieces of the puzzle all fell into place." Or, as an engineer said, "It's kind of making a fusion right there. I recall that suddenly seeing the situation, it catalyzed."

This is the "aha" of discovery experiences. One can have all the facts, but fail to put them together in a way that makes a meaningful picture. It still requires that moment of imagination or insight to form them into a new framework. Bill had that moment during an experience of discrimination.

It was just unbelievable. I had experienced something in the South, but I was really too young to really put those things into any kind of perspective. For example, I went into a store one time to get a drink of water, and there was a white fountain and a

colored fountain. The colored fountain in this particular dime store was really nothing—it amounted to a pipe with fungus growing out of it. I wasn't about to drink out of that thing. And I went over to the other fountain, and the lady raced over saying "You go down and drink out of the little faucet." I said, "No way, lady." She was going to call the police and have us hauled off to jail. And I said, "Forget you," and I ran out of the store.

To go down to a place and sit down and get ready to have something to eat. Somebody says, "Well, I'm sorry but we don't serve blacks here." Or the fact that there was one white girl who used to hang around with my wife. Do you know they had the Ku Klux Klan chasing me because we had become friends?

Or the fact that when you would go to a movie the black guy was portrayed as "Yas suh, boss" with a handkerchief around his neck. And when I was overseas in the service, the Rumanians were just as dark as we were. They didn't want to come to this country because they would be identified as blacks. And then the Rumanian girls would flop with the white guys, but the black guys were "out there." They didn't have a chance. Ridiculous.

I think I was aware of all those things. But it wasn't until later that I began to connect.

A handful of persons interviewed had lived abroad at some time. Jeff said, "I think your attitude toward your own country changes very much by living outside of it." Not only did attitudes change because the U.S. is interpreted differently from abroad, but because while abroad, people were often confronted with more intense expressions of human misery.

We were in Mexico. There were beggars, adults in poverty. But then you notice children in poverty. At casket makers' places, you notice there are almost as many caskets for children as there are for adults. Then you begin to say, "Aha—the child mortality rate." There are lots of little things like this that start you thinking.

Jeff has returned to the Third World to work full time for humanization and justice. The casket incident was a start-you-thinking moment, later followed by dozens of other moving experiences.

4. "It was an awakening" and "It was an illuminating experience" are metaphors describing opening a window or shining a light in the mind. Many of the coming-to-awareness experiences can be likened to the creation of a window in the mind. An opening is created so that the person begins to see something that was there all the time, but just not seen. "For the first time I saw." "All of a sudden you could see." "I began to notice." Feminists refer to the click experience in which suddenly a light goes on in one's head. Cartoonists show light bulbs lighting up over people's heads. "My eyes were opened" sometimes refers to a new insight or interpretation—sometimes to a new sensitization.

Figure Four

Steffens describes the moment when he had that great flash of insight that reordered his own moral perception about the nature of evil in society. The moment occurs when a former railway magnate, then mayor of Cleveland, tries to convince Steffens that the problem of corrupt politics does not really lie with corrupt politicians or businessmen per se—that in their private lives, they are quite good people.

> "It's those who seek privileges who corrupt, it's those who possess privileges that defend our corrupt politics. Can't you see that?"
> This was more like a flash of light than a speech, and as I took it in and shed it around in my head, he added, "It is privilege that causes evil in the world, not wickedness; and not men."[19]

It was like a flash of light penetrating the walls of Steffens' mind. But the break in the walls was so new, so unexpected, that he had to shine a flashlight around to see what light it shed on other things lying around there.

5. "Getting it in focus" is like the alignment of previously incongruent frames. In this case it is not so much that separate pieces suddenly come together, but that incongruent, overlapping experiences become newly aligned to form a congruent whole.

To draw again from Lincoln Steffens:

> One day Upton Sinclair called me at the office of *McClure's* and remonstrated.
> "What you report," he said, "is enough to make a complete picture of the system, but you seem not to see it. Don't you see it? Don't you see what you are showing?" . . .
> What Sinclair did not realize was that I could hardly believe what I was seeing, and that I could not, in so short a time, change my mind to fit the new picture. I was not yet over my education; so I had my two pictures, one on top of the other, on the canvas of my mind. I needed time to adjust my imagination to the facts as they were, not more experience, but time. . . .[20]

Steffens had two pictures (or frames) in his mind. He had trouble adjusting the old one to the new one. In other cases, the distinction may not be old picture versus new picture, but a group of overlapping experiences that don't quite come into focus as one single picture—a sort of astigmatism of consciousness. In either case, the coming-to-awareness experience is one in which the several frames become congruent.

Those participants who felt the change brewing for a long time experienced a set of overlapping and contradictory feelings that remained incoherent. Sometimes one part of the picture would prevail, sometimes another. Or perhaps the whole scheme was so diffuse and unfocused that it did not quite form a single picture. At some point, an experience provided an ordering principle, a focal point that suddenly led to the emergence of a coherent meaning.

Thus far, the coming-together or getting-it-in-focus experiences have been referred to as though they only concerned gaining insight or a new interpretive perspective. These metaphors may also be used to describe the creation of what

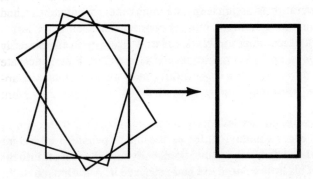

Figure Five

might be called an existential frame, or a frame filled with meaning. It is possible to have insight without an accompanying passion or passion without appropriate insight. "You may intellectually verbalize racial equality. But you don't in your deep down part feel that way."

> When the cognitive meaning of an object changes for a subject, the perceptual adjustment will be much smaller than when the moral meaning changes, for changes in moral meaning are accompanied by changes in affect toward the object, while changes in cognitive meaning seldom are.[21]

In cases of rape, many women go through a stage in which they describe the rape in a super-rational, almost detached, manner. The experience was so powerful that for a time they have to set emotion aside; if the experience were fully constituted, it would be more than they could deal with.

Emotional arousal is a sine qua non of existential awareness—awareness that goes beyond intellectual acknowledgment that something is true. In perception one sees a problem for the first time; in interpretation one gives it a certain meaningful shape—moral shape in this case. In emotion, one's awareness is linked into the lived reality of one's embodiment: "I was devastated." "It made me angry."

An existential frame is one in which perception, interpretation, and emotion become congruent—one sees, understands, feels, and finally acts. It is possible, like Bill, to experience discrimination, but at the time, lack a framework of interpretation to assign it any meaning other than just suffering. One can see something, but not connect that seeing to a larger pattern of meaning until later. Harold grew up in the South in the 1940s and 1950s. He recalls a moment that generated discomfort, but which was insufficient to trigger a change, given his white southern upbringing at the time.

The white folks would play baseball there at the little country school every Sunday. A lot of the black people would come around and watch the game. Somebody fouled a ball off into the trees. This little colored kid had retrieved it. And Don asked the kid to give him the ball. The little colored kid—it was an incredibly audacious thing to do—said, "Give me two bits first." Don killed him. Pulled out a knife and killed him. A little kid. Nothing was done. Not a goddamned thing was done.

People talked about it and would say, "You know it was an awful thing that Don did. He shouldn't have done that." But there was never a question of calling him up before a judge and saying, "You son of a bitch. You're going to jail." The fact that nothing was done wasn't even questioned. And I didn't question it either. I was impressed. Obviously that made a real impression on me. But no one questioned why nothing was done.

Harold saw the killing; the experience stuck in his consciousness. But it was only later when he acquired a framework of interpretation different from that of his youth that the event became congruent with his life.

Jack describes himself as "once-born," as having grown up in a family where conversations about political events were dished up with the bacon and eggs. Even so, he recalls a quickening experience when the racism he had already heard about came alive or existential to him—emotion joined knowledge.

One of the early appropriations of this into my life was the time when I can remember going with another buddy to the tri-county fair. We stuck by one barker who was trying to get a crowd around for something. He picked out a little black boy about seven or eight years old to come up and stand with him. He

began trying to talk with him. The boy was obviously shy and not wanting to do this, but the white man said, "Come over here and I'll give you something," and he waved a dollar bill at him.

The boy couldn't resist and got a little closer and finally stood by him. The barker began ridiculing him. "Well, you're barefooted. Don't you have any shoes?" And the boy said, "Well, yeah, but we only wear them in the wintertime when we need to." And the barker began cracking jokes and things that got a crowd. Then when he got the crowd there he said, "Now boy, I promised to give you something and I'm sure gonna do that." He pulled out a little rubber doll and gave it to him and put the dollar in his pocket. It was an outrage to me. I think that was the first time that I can recall sensing personally the outrage of discrimination. That was probably not a conversion, but more of an accepting into my own life some things I'd heard in the family.

Those coming-to-awareness experiences that are more than just the discovery of a new way of viewing things and have a strong emotional component, create frames deep with existential meaning. They are more than just windows of perception. They are internalized at a physical, gut level. They are existential frames of an embodied consciousness, rooted not only in one's mind, but in one's body. "I have found that catastrophes are only real when one reaches out, grabs you personally by the throat and screams in your face."[22] The experiences can be emotionally compelling: "It lit my fire."

It may be for this reason that people use embodiment-related metaphors to describe these experiences. The effects of the experiences not only changed their minds, but changed their lives in some cases. It is as though the experiences are imprinted on the skeletal frame and viscera that bind and interrelate with consciousness. The alignment of perception, emotion and interpretation creates a thick congruent reality in their ongoing lives.

This analysis suggests that these existential meaning frames contain the symbol systems of our autobiographies, which sort out the real from the unreal. In an existential moment we discover "I am me," "I am really going to die," or "Her suffering hurts her like my suffering hurts me." The existential moments constitute frames of reference that fix our inner sense of the really good, true, and lovely—our way of attending to meaning and being.

Unfortunately, a deeply held existential frame does not necessarily widen into a picture window, or a glass wall in one's mind. Some people who were concerned about race just couldn't get excited about Vietnam, and vice versa. Some minorities can see the discrimination that other minorities suffer through the window of their own discrimination experience, but are not moved by the other group's pain.

Jack was active in racial concerns, took some dramatic personal and professional risks in the fifties and sixties. Though he had been a conscientious objector in World War II, he was only marginally involved in the anti-war movement in the Vietnam era. He explained that he couldn't do everything, and had decided to focus on race. The racial issue had grasped him at an existential level, which made it a thicker reality than some other social concerns (although he was involved in many other concerns at lesser levels). So, frames may exist in various degrees of clarity, liveliness, or comprehensiveness, with the most powerful arising in symbolic moments.

Evidence from Other Sources

C. Wright Mills suggests that one way of drawing out the inner aspects of a phenomenon is to look at its parallels and opposites. The closest parallel to accidentally occasioned changes of consciousness is forced changes of consciousness—brainwashing.

The term "brainwashing" became current during the Korean conflict. The term itself is interesting. It suggests that one's brain is wiped clean—back to the tabula rasa—so that it then can be filled with new perceptions. Other terms used to describe this phenomenon are thought reform, ideological remolding, and coercive persuasion.

One author describes the steps in brainwashing as (1) unfreezing, (2) changing, and (3) refreezing. In the first step, the "existing equilibrium is no longer stable." The second step is "seeing the light," or coming to awareness of the new model or beliefs. The third step entails a "reintegration of the new equilibrium into the rest of the personality."[23] This description closely parallels the formal stages found in our interviews where experiences occurred serendipitously.

Robert Jay Lifton carried out various studies, trying to document the psychological effects of dramatic social changes. He studied the survivors of Hiroshima, brainwashing in Korea, and United States Vietnam veterans, especially those present at the My Lai massacre.

In his discussion of brainwashing, Lifton stakes out a middle ground between the traditional psychiatrists who believe that little lasting change happens after patterns are formed in infancy, and the brainwashers who believe they can bring total change. "Change during adult life is real and perpetual; significant change may be extremely difficult to consolidate."[24]

Lifton applies what he learned in his studies of brainwashing to open, personal change, the process by which people make spontaneous changes. It is a three-step sequence—confrontation (unfreezing), reordering (changing), and renewal (refreezing). This triad suggests the same structure and dynamic of consciousness as the interviews—confrontation and collapse of a frame, reordering the picture inside, and then the constitution of a new frame.

Lifton recalls a specific moment when his own consciousness toward the Vietnam war was changed. He uses the same sort of metaphors found in the interviews, and like many of our participants, locates the event in a specific time and place. Even though he had talked with survivors of Hiroshima and Korean brainwashing,

> My Lai shocked nonetheless, in its concrete details and its dimensions. It brought about an abrupt change in my own relationship to the war, and in my life in general. I recall the shame and rage I experienced when reading an early account of My Lai in the *New York Times* in November, 1969, (while on an airplane taking me to Toronto for a talk on psycho-history and a radio broadcast on nuclear weapons).[25]

In his subsequent study on returning veterans, Lifton documents the opposite of sensitization, namely, the desensitization the soldiers experienced. It began with their training, continued through days of slogging through extreme heat and humidity, and was reinforced by language that reduced human beings to "gooks." The soldiers started out as John Waynes and Boy Scouts, but their psyches became numbed through the progressive brutalization depicted so graphically in the movies, *The Deer Hunter* and *Apocalypse Now*. One day, there was a "first death" in the company—it became the turning point. " 'Suddenly we realized a guy could get killed out there. So let's get our revenge before we go.' "[26] Their psychological shift was described in the same words as that of the interview participants, except that the soldiers' hearts were (as it was said of Pharaoh) hardened. The change qua change was similar in structure, although the results were different.

Killing piled upon killing until it became " 'like scratching an itch . . . it's going to drive you nuts unless you do it.' " Fear and frenzy drove them to kill even small children, and then again demonstrate the enormous capacity of the human mind to rationalize whatever it is disposed to—" 'Well, they'll grow up [to help the VC].' "[27]

The structure of change of consciousness suggested in this chapter receives further support from Thomas Kuhn and others' interpretations of the nature of scientific discovery. Kuhn's description of change of paradigms in scientific revolutions parallels our description of frame changes, which suggests both are grounded in the structure of consciousness itself.

Kuhn says that scientific inquiry in an era or within a discipline is characterized by the pervasiveness of a model, or a paradigm that serves "for a time implicitly to define the legitimate problems and methods of a research field."[28] When newly discovered facts do not fit the paradigm, adjustments are made. However, the basic paradigm stays intact, even if it means the new facts have to be explained away. A given paradigm may hold sway for centuries, setting the basic frame of reference within which scientific endeavors take place.

Change of paradigms does not occur by the simple process of the cumulation of new evidence. "Discovery commences with the awareness of anomaly, i.e., with the recognition that nature has somehow violated the paradigm-induced expectations that govern normal science."[29]

The awareness that leads to a change of paradigm occurs in a flash of insight, in which the whole nature of the problem is reconceived—an old frame is broken down and a new one is created. The transition does not come by the simple addition of more "facts," but entails "a reconstruction of the field from new fundamentals." Kuhn notes Herbert Butterfield's description of a paradigm change as " 'picking up the other end of the stick,' a process that involves 'handling the same bundle of data as before, but placing them in a new system of relations with one another by giving them a different framework.' "[30]

Kuhn also likens the discovery process to Gestalt perception experiments where the picture that first looks like a bird now looks like an antelope, or a Gestalt card experiment where people are asked to identify a series of playing cards—some cards are normal and others are changed into, for example, a black four of hearts. People identify a *black* four of *hearts* as either the four of spades or the four of hearts, without seeing the incongruity. It is not until they are repeatedly shown the cards that their normal expectations are disrupted, and they discover the difference. Some respondents never see the anomaly.

Kuhn suggests that:

> Either as a metaphor or because it reflects the nature of the mind, that psychological experiment provides a wonderfully simple and cogent schema for the process of scientific discovery. In science, as in the playing card experiment, novelty emerges only with difficulty, manifested by resistance, against a background provided by expectation. Initially, only the anticipated and usual are experienced . . . awareness of anomaly opens a period in which conceptual categories are adjusted until the initially anomalous has become the anticipated. At this point the discovery has been completed.[31]

Sometimes a paradigm shift instigates a crisis in science. The change of paradigm modifies the meaning of both explained and unexplained facts in the old paradigm. Paradigm shifts are changes in world view. They create a fundamental orientation to the phenomena of the scientist's interest. It is interesting that when scientists describe these moments of discovery they sometimes use the same metaphors that individuals use in describing their changes of consciousness. One of Kuhn's footnotes cites an article describing a major shift in theoretical physics—"The Turning Point."[32]

Significant changes of consciousness in individuals and societies are something more than changes of worldview. They are changes in the assignment of meaning to an event, in which intellectual, emotional, and physical orientation shift. Getting it fully in focus is more than changing a lens. It is changing one's relation to the event.

MORAL INSIGHT

Many different kinds of frame-change occur; some have nothing directly to do with morality. A person may suddenly begin to see the world in aesthetic or religious terms. Among moral changes, some are toward the good, others bad. The writings of Lifton and others suggest that under the right circumstances, many intelligent and decent people would push small children into gas chambers or machine-gun them down. That sounds harsh, but so is the reality of fifty-seven children dying every minute of hunger and hunger-related diseases, which doesn't seem to bother us that much.

We need to know not only how a frame changes, but about the moral picture inside the frame. One corner of that picture is the participants' view that they have become more moral through the change. They experience the change as being a turnabout—progression and growth (both personal and moral), moving from closed to open, sleeping to waking. Even if they later feel they have drifted from the seminal moments of change, they sense that drifting as a moral loss.

Moral Growth

These changes are experienced as *turnabouts,* as movements around turning points. The degree of turn may vary widely. "It turned my head around" may mean a 180-degree change in awareness. "It changed my life" is considerably more serious. But even the person who experiences a smaller arc of turning begins to look in a different direction and see things not seen before.

The word traditionally used to describe major changes of consciousness is "conversion." To con-vert is to turn with, to turn together, to turn from one position, state, or direction to another. It is to become the con-verse of what one was before the change. Conversions occur at the turning points of life.

Partly because the word "conversion" has heavy religious connotations, Peter Berger uses the word "alternation" to describe such changes. Alternation suggests an oscillation—a turning back and forth—of consciousness. There is, he says, "the possibility that an individual may alternate back and forth between logically contradictory meaning systems."[1] I have referred sometimes to my research as a study of moral alternation—the switching of moral worlds.

Berger and Luckmann describe alternation as a complete or radical shift of subjective meaning. They even provide a recipe.

> A "recipe" for successful alternation has to include both social and conceptual conditions, the social . . . serving as the matrix of the conceptual. The most important social condition is the availability of an effective plausibility structure, that is, a social base serving as the "laboratory" of transformation.[2]

The change, they say, is mediated by significant others with whom one "must establish strongly affective identification." . . . "These significant others are the guides into the new reality."[3] When one has passed through a successful alternation, one reinterprets one's past history. In order for the transformation to be sustained, one needs to associate with people who hold the new vision of reality.

Sometimes I was able to identify a moral mentor associated with the alternation experience, but not always. Most of the participants found as new conversation partners other socially involved people who helped them solidify and sustain their new stance, but this was not always true either. A few people hung on tenaciously to their new orientation, even though the milieu in which they found themselves was surging in the opposite direction. Such conversation partners as they had, were friends in other places who shared their values, but with whom they talked for the most part only in memory and imagination.

Alternation is a better word than conversion to describe these changes. It catches the mobility of a consciousness, that switches or slides back and forth. As people change through new experiences, so do their views of good and bad, right and wrong.

The description that more than any other picks up the character of change-of-consciousness as an alternation, a switching back and forth of moral worlds, occurred when Joe mused nostalgically over the dimming of his own racial awareness. He draws on spatial metaphors to describe his experience.

Now, I wonder how much of a transformation did take place in my life. That's a question that I'm increasingly having to deal with. It's kind of interesting. I think I had a genuine change experience. But I'm not so sure that I haven't changed back in a lot of ways.

Certainly a lot of the consciousness that I had in the past I don't have now. Certainly a lot of the attitudes I had in the past I don't have now. And yet I do have a feeling of knowing what it's like to feel the other way. I keep thinking of the song "Toyland"—Once you pass its boundaries, you may never enter again.

But yes, you always have those experiences, you know. You go through something. Yet it's always back there ready, and in a sense you can go back. You can switch back and instantly you can pick up on what it had felt to be there in the past.

Even though his awareness is not as lively as it once was, he senses that he cannot go all the way back to where he was before the changes. He knows that his awareness is still there, at some level, ready to be tapped into anew. Probably there are many people like him in American society who are not very active, but who carry symbolic meanings inside themselves that one day may be quickened anew. Their fully constituted existential frames may have thinned out, but have not disappeared.

Turnabouts have moral significance. The person is turning away from lack of awareness and apathy to concern and action—turning toward a moral context. The changes are not just neutral; they are turns toward viewing the world in moral terms.

Another set of metaphors indicating both change and moral growth are those describing *small steps and quantum leaps*— metaphors of motion through space. Some arrived at awareness by taking a host of small steps or traveling little roads, while others spoke of dramatic leaps forward.

Gwyn: "Perhaps there are so many different small steps that it's hard to say, 'Oh, I had an awakening, or revelation.' I frankly do not think I did. There are moments that stand out perhaps a little bit more than others." Margie: "I sort of evolved into it rather than having a click type of thing." Barbara: "There hasn't been a quantum leap. I've added a whole bunch of data as I've gone along."

They and others describe the gradualness of their moral journey—using terms like "little roads," the "once-born," "small steps," "evolved," "grew." These metaphors emphasize the linearity of their journey, and the basic continuity of their consciousness as it traveled along. Many spoke of their continuity with the values learned at home, or the example shown by their parents. Jorge's comments are typical of those who see themselves as having taken many small steps. But even he recalls one symbolic moment, which stood out among the others.

There haven't been any big magical leaps. In a lot of senses you've got some kinds of basic understanding that you've grown up with from way back. I didn't have a Damascus-road experience. How many of us do? We have little roads.

When I was a kid, man, I was one of those kids that was always speaking English. There was a lady who was running for student council secretary on the white ticket, and I was campaign manager for the blue ticket. I made a campaign speech about I'm not sure that we want to have such and such a person elected to our student council office because they have to represent us at functions at other high schools, and this person speaks English

with an accent. We don't want to have this kind of person talking for us, man.

That's a lot of indoctrination to come up with that kind of statement. I made the transition from making that kind of statement three or four years later. I had no social awareness. Had I voted in 1960 I would have voted for Nixon. I mean I wasn't anywhere in terms of social awareness.

Later there was an incident that I single out now as something that I can look at symbolically, you know. It was down on the south side. And I'd walk around the neighborhood. And walking around bumping into old friends sitting on the corners, and just seeing the decay, the slums there. And it's ten years now and just seeing it there and saying, "Hey, man. This ain't no good! This ain't no good!"

Jorge really did change. It's just that the change incidents were not individually experienced as having been momentous. He could go back and pick out one incident symbolizing the variety of experiences that had affected him. Even that one was not terribly earthshaking. Many small experiences cumulatively create change and growth.

Other persons speak of their changes in more dramatic terms. Karen's breakthrough changed her life. It was a turnabout; she made a quantum leap. Because she is so articulate, and because this interview contains many helpful hints about change experiences, moral consciousness, and activation, she will be quoted at length.

Well, I did make some jumps in my life. I came from a very conservative background, grew up in a small town, voted for Goldwater in '64, voted for Nixon in '68, and between '68 and '72, made a tremendous turnabout and got involved in the women's movement. I drastically reassessed my marriage and got out of it, and then decided to go to a professional school. I've made some important readjustments in my life.

I grew up out in a little town in western Wisconsin. My folks ran a business there. They were politically conservative, as most everybody there was. And I accepted those views right up until I was in my late twenties. I married when I was eighteen and an undergraduate. The man I married was also very conservative and seven years older than I was. It was a very traditional arrangement. He was a strong, dominating, parental figure.

I was married eleven years. During all that time I remained politically conservative and accepted a traditional life pattern. He moved into a profession. We bought a house in the suburbs and got ready to start a family. I taught high school and then went back and got some graduate degrees. But during that time I accepted all of the conventional wisdom about how one lives one's life without questioning it seriously at all, even though during that time there was a tremendous amount of frustration with the marriage. I was teaching and I was going to graduate school, but in the marriage I was very frustrated. Even though we were both working, I would always come home and do the meals, and do the house, and bear the burden of responsibility for getting all the trivia done. And when I didn't, I would get upset about this and feel it wasn't fair. And when Roy would criticize, "Why aren't my shirts back from the laundry?" or whatever, I would be angry with him for criticizing me.

Part of me would rebel and say, "Why is it I have to be the one responsible for getting your shirts back from the laundry?" And yet I couldn't come out and say that, or when I would try to I would simply dissolve in tears, because I had such conflicts about it. On the one hand I had simply accepted the fact that it *was* my responsibility and felt that I had this *moral obligation*, unquestioned, simply because I didn't understand them at all. So that anytime I did try to broach the subject, all I could do was cry, because I didn't know how to handle it.

So the woman's movement was a godsend for me in that it articulated things that I couldn't articulate for myself. I read *The Feminine Mystique*. And it just crystallized for me all these feelings that for eight to ten years of marriage had been building up that I couldn't articulate—that I was afraid to look at directly.

But why was I afraid to look at it directly? I don't know. It was because all the power that I had been brought up to respect was on the side of my behaving properly, of my doing these things, and I was afraid of that power. All the power said "You do these things." To question was to challenge that sort of thing. We simply accept that power, that authority. We're afraid to challenge it.

So I hadn't questioned it, and *The Feminine Mystique* sort of did that for me and helped me make that quantum leap, you know—by golly, no wonder I was mad! It *was* unfair! It confirmed those feelings that I had always repressed. It wasn't right. No wonder I was resentful. So it helped me articulate what it was that had been bothering me for years, and accept the fact that I didn't have to feel guilty for being angry—that I had every reason to be angry.

Actually I went much further than she went in that book. It was like she just made the first step, and once I recognized the first step, then two, three, four and five became clear. I recognized quickly that the book hadn't gone nearly far enough. And so I began reading everything I could find on the subject. And for months I just absorbed all the feminist literature that was just beginning to come out at that time, about 1970. And finally by that spring, I really had put it together. It took me months of absorbing the stuff before I could act on it.

Finally when I did I was ready to say, "Okay this is wrong!" The structure that Roy and I had in our marriage was wrong, and we couldn't live with it. It was immoral to live that way. And then I began aggressively trying to make a change.

In the women's movement there wasn't anything happening in our city at that time. But that summer we organized a state chapter of the Women's Action League. And I went to the first meeting and was elected to an office.

We quickly became active. We immediately began our first investigation of city banks and filed charges against them. And so this helped me to focus all that energy which was, you know, really right on the surface. I was badly needing some kind of outlet. That's a whole different chapter of what that did for me—having to pull it together and develop as a person.

The turnabout, I think, began with reading *The Feminine Mystique,* and that giving me the courage to put some things together and to take the next steps. There was another incident in there that was peculiarly important, even though on the surface it sounds rather trivial. I was taking my Ph.D. comprehensives at the time. They are given in sections. I failed the one that was my strongest subject, which I knew better than any of the other areas I had to be tested on. I failed it, and that was a shocker. I'd made straight A's through graduate school, always been a top student, and I failed that subject.

Well, it was a real blow to my ego. But more importantly when I talked to the professor about why I had failed it, the reasons turned out to be so irrational. And I took it again a few months later and passed it. But the revelation to me was that I was so shocked that sometimes people fail for things that aren't their own fault. For a WASP, that's a very important lesson. It's something you can get through life without even realizing. You know, when the doors are open for you, you don't realize that sometimes they've closed for people for reasons that they have no control over.

And somehow that experience focused that for me, the same time as getting into the women's movement, that sometimes you fail for something you can't help—that has nothing to do with ability. There are blocks thrown up in your way that you can't control, and that most of us who are white and middle class don't recognize. Not just for women, but for minorities and also for people who have handicaps they can't control. So the combination of those two experiences did a lot for me.

The most immediate point is Karen's sense of having made a dramatic turnabout or a quantum leap forward in her life. Her change-of-interpretation is almost classic. She thought of herself as blameworthy for not getting Roy's shirts back from the laundry. She was not only at fault, it was a moral failure—failure of an obligation imposed by the society by virtue of her role, and accepted by her as right. It was not that her situation changed; it was her interpretation of the situation that changed. *The Feminine Mystique* enabled her to reorganize the meaning of what was happening. Failing her exam led to another change of interpretation, and an insight that no cause-and-effect analysis could have predicted—"People fail for things that aren't their own fault." This personal hurt was translated into understanding and concern for the situation of other people.

Dag Hammarskjöld uses the word *Vägmärken (Markings)* to profile his life. The book was originally a diary—not the sort that chronicles the mundane events of everyday life, but one in which events and reflections too important to be lost in the cluttered closets of memory are tagged for retrieval. His writings record his inner sense of meaning, rather than the public events for which he was known. "These notes?—They were signposts you began to set up after you had reached a point where you needed them, a fixed point that was on no account to be lost sight of. And so they have remained."[4]

Vägmärken—Markings, Trailmarks, or *Signposts* as the book might have been titled—are recorded as significant meaning-places of a person's life. Both those who took one step at a time, and those who made big leaps might have identified with the notion of markings or signposts. For they too had experiences sufficiently significant to be thought of as milestones, or as having pointed their lives in lasting directions.

Many people experience the change as movement from *closed to open.* The moral symbolism evoked in these spatial metaphors seems more dramatic than in the case of the repositioning metaphors. The person was locked in, in a cage, trapped, half-bound, in a corner, in a white box. After the change he or she was free, more open, had widened horizons. "It opened up a whole new world for me." It may be that the human notion of freedom is an implicate of the human experience of space. When we want to take away someone's freedom, the first thing we do is bind or limit that person's space to a room or cell. The pragmatic necessities of keeping the person bound dictate some of this—it is easier to guard or control someone whose mobility is severely limited. The significance of these limiting and binding acts may be much deeper than pragmatic necessities would imply. It may have to do with our sense of space, perhaps even an inner satisfaction that those whom we would punish cannot move their bodies through space with freedom. The relations between freedom and our experience of space are tantalizing, though they cannot be pursued here.

It is not accidental that Christi furnished a den so it would not remind her of the state she had moved to and that she did not want the Realtor to take a Polaroid picture of them in front of the house. Nor is it accidental that gay persons speak of "coming out of a closet," or "crossing a boundary." One of the most pervasive aspects of our experience of life has to do with the way we experience spaces. That sense of spatiality is projected in metaphors and images with which we express our inner sense of our experience.

Toward the end of some of the interviews, we asked some participants to "draw a picture of yourself before and after the change." Karen's response:

Well, before, I see some good things in myself in terms of a kind of innocence and goodwill, but also a tremendous amount of fear. My life was basically circumscribed by fear. And part of that growing self-awareness was overcoming all the fears that we're all subject to. The only way to be alive is to overcome as many fears as possible. The women's movement helped me overcome a lot of fears. It's helped me open a lot of doors that I was afraid to open before.

In drawing a picture I see myself as sort of shrunken in, defensively afraid of getting out of a very narrow little room—afraid to look outside. And now I see myself as striding around a number of rooms, not nearly all of the rooms that are available and not near enough sky, but at least much less of the defensive posture and much more room to work in.

I came out of such narrow, white middle-class experiences and values. The women's movement made me much more sensitive to discrimination of all sorts—for example that people fail for reasons that they have no control over. I became very interested and curious to know what everyone else's lives were like. The direction I feel I have to go now is learning more about that.

It's like we've deprived so much of ourselves. We live in an enormous house, in an enormous countryside, with an enormous sky. And we live in a closet all our lives because we don't know anything more than just this tiny little thing. And growing means learning about everybody else's life too because that's your life, Somehow it's all your life too. And the only way to get in touch with yourself is to know what everybody else has. They give you part of yourself back.

The image of the sky comes to me, seems right, but I'm not sure I can articulate what it means. It's as if the sky would be God, the All. The house is our prison. And somehow we have to get out of the house. Opening up the doors to the house is the first step. But somehow complete perfection—complete self-fulfillment—in some way, is getting to the sky.

I'm not sure I can articulate very clearly what the sky is. It's just the sense that the house is a restriction that is very difficult to get away from. Most all you can do is enlarge the house. But somehow the goal is the sky. That's what we're seeking is to get the roof off or get the hell out the front door. That's very difficult to do, and maybe that's the state of pure sainthood or nirvana. It's the sky which is very difficult to reach.

I've been talking a lot about my own increasing freedom as a person, maybe not enough about the sense of ties with other people that went along with that. The sense of belonging in a real sense to all kinds of humanity and having those terribly important human ties that makes me part of all aspects of society. And somehow that all comes together. My personal sense of freedom is tied into also to that sense of belonging and being responsible for, being a part of, all those other parts of humanity that I had really been ignorant of before. Somehow that goes together and I'm not sure just how, the sense of all of us being a piece.

It was really brought home last weekend. I flew to San Francisco and spent a lovely week with a Hispanic family. And then I got on the plane to come back, and this guy sat down next to me. And he starts talking about how people abuse the welfare system and this conventional crap. I was just trying to communicate with him. This poor man. I know where he comes from. I've been there too, but how ignorant. The narrowness of his life—that closet. He's never even looked out the window to see what's really going on out there because the only people he knows are people who live in that same closet who've not looked outside. Somehow that experience was jolting.

Closets, cages, caves, prisons, restrictions, shadows, shrunken in and narrowness—versus enormity, windows, the sky, nirvana, fulfillment, the light, freedom, and being a part of other people. We see gains in freedom, self-confidence, openness to other people's unique individuality, and a sense of connectedness to them. These descriptions have a moral tone, are perceived by Karen to have constituted moral growth. It seems contentious to argue with this self-evaluation. That is not to say that other people who find their inner movement narrowing rather than opening—seeking comfort rather than openness—are less moral. Rather for Karen and those around her, the movement seems transparently good.

Karen's words leap from metaphor to symbol as spaces take on symbolic meaning. We return to symbolic spaces, if not physically, then in memory to recover the meaning that is there for us. John Howard Griffin imaginatively returned inside the rooms to put himself in touch with the meaning that experience had for his life. The exploration of the significant "sites of our intimate lives" is part of the archaeology of our inmost meanings.[5]

Perception and Interpretation

The movement of consciousness is also experienced as a change from *sleeping to waking,* blindness to sight, dark to light. "The light dawned; it opened my eyes; I became aware." These metaphors express a subtle evaluation that one was, prior to the change, awake without being aware, looking without seeing. The changed state is evaluated as better seeing or real seeing, over against the earlier state—now seen as moral blindness, drowsiness, or pseudo-awakeness.

To perceive is to be able to receive images. The person who has made a turnabout or gone from closed to open is attuned to new possibilities, thus better able to receive images. The receipt of images is not some sort of crude imprinting; it entails inner receptivity, an openness to reception, and a preparedness to face and assimilate them. Images may cumulate alongside of others, connect with preestablished patterns, change frames, or reach into the hidden depths of a person's inner self. The act of perceiving is intrinsically an interpretive act.

Perception is not just passive openness to images; it is a reaching-out toward the possible—not just light streaming through a window, but a peering out of that window. This looking out can occur across a narrow or wide spectrum, and with varying degrees of intensity. A person may put a question to a setting and inquire something of it. Once we begin to see the world in moral terms, we may continually put the moral question to new settings, or—to change the metaphor—once we have acquired a moral lens, we may hold it to our eye to view old and new settings in a moral light.

Margie: All you've got to do is open your eyes and ears, and you know that there's all kinds of inequity and discrepancies. When the school system is failing, when the political system is failing, when health services are lacking, welfare services are lacking—all you've got to do is open your eyes. It's clearly there. Now the question is, why is it that some people see that and internalize it, whereas other people don't, even though they've been in the same setting?

The act of perception is an active negotiation between the self and the setting. We look or avert our eyes. There is willing-to-see as there is willing-to-do. Sustained seeing is a decision, a judgment, about the worthiness of the seen.

Many instances of choosing not to see could be cited. Germans who lived in Munich really did not want to see (know) what was going on at Dachau. When someone is told about the enormity and intensity of human suffering in the Third World or the other America, that one may say, "I don't want to know about it." Participants in the Milgram experiment who believed they were administering a painful shock to an innocent stranger were in one experimental condition placed so they could see the victim. "Subjects frequently averted their eyes from the person they were shocking, often turning their heads in an awkward and conspicuous manner. One subject explained, 'I didn't want to see the consequences of what I had done.' " (Nonetheless, some who refused to look at the victim continued to administer shocks.)[6]

The act of perception can be a sort of appreciative or concerned leaning-toward something—waiting for it to unfold or reveal itself. As inner seeing, perception includes the act of constructing and internalizing the meaning of what is seen.

The paths of life cross one another at many points. One meets innumerable beings. But there are few whom one "sees" in the ethical sense, few to whom one gives the sympathetic glance—one might almost say the loving glance, for the glance that appreciates value is loving. And, conversely, how few are they by whom one in turn is "seen"! Worlds meet, surface lightly grazes surface, in their depth they remain untouched and solitary; and they part again. Or for a lifetime or more they run parallel, externally united, perhaps chained to one another, and yet each one remains locked out from the other.[7]

One sees the surface or the inner meaning. Continuing to look begins one's formulation of a relationship toward a setting, including the other person who is part of that setting. It is positioning oneself toward or away from a setting, to negotiate where I stand in relation to what is at hand. Perception is evaluative. Perception of other people is intrinsically moral. Edward Tiryakian's notion of an Assumptive Frame of Reference initiated the discussion of frames and frame changes. Tiryakian suggests that perceptual frames are intrinsically moral.

> Perception, as a transaction between the AFR and external reality, has the important quality of being *morally evaluative* of what it perceives; the ordering and evaluating particularly of social objects is at the same time a *consciousness of* and a *conscience of* them.[8]

He explains that to be aware (conscious) of one's neighbor is, at the same time, to perceive the neighbor in a certain morally evaluative light—as trustworthy, criminal, or whatever.

The notion of a frame as morally evaluative can be extended. A frame organizes the world in moral terms. To turn our knowing glance toward or away from some reality is a moral act. To see or not to see, is a preconscious moral commitment. If I do not see suffering in a world of starving people, if I do not see racism where it is virulent—that is already a moral ordering of the world, although a preconscious one.

A person who routinely perceives the world in moral terms is one who is sensitized, morally aware. A moral frame of reference is a frame through which one intends with care toward a world perceived as intrinsically social, comprised of people (and nature) who (and which) in meaningful respects are like-me, yet not-me. To intend with care is to care about, be appreciative of, and assign priority in seeing and doing to moral dimensions of the social and natural world. It is to view the human world in moral and aesthetic terms first, not residually. It means putting the questions, "Is it good? is it beautiful?" to the multiple contexts of one's lived engagements. Perception and interpretation of the world as a moral phenomenon is requisite to taking the responsibility that leads a person to act in behalf of the common good.

Every action in a setting is predicated on an interpretation of what is happening there. Behavioral studies have explored many factors related to people's interpretation of a setting—a person is more likely to help someone who has fallen to the sidewalk with an apparent heart attack, than someone who appears to be a chronic alcoholic. One crucial factor in how people respond to an emergency is whether or not they interpret it to be an emergency. Studies have demonstrated that people are more likely to respond if other people around them seem to be interpreting the situation as an emergency. They use other people to check out their own interpretation.[9]

Albert Camus dramatically portrayed the difference that a mistake in interpretation can make in *The Stranger*.[10] The leading character kills a man in a confusing set of exchanges, although it is never clear they have any reason to be enemies—just strangers. As he sits in jail awaiting trial, he finds a piece of yellowed newspaper on the underside of his straw mattress.

The clipping tells the story of a person who leaves home to make his way in the world. After a quarter of a century he returns to his old home to surprise his mother and sister with his new wealth and family. To make the surprise complete, he books his wife and child into one hotel and goes to stay at the modest inn run by his mother and sister. He uses an assumed name, and they fail to recognize him after so long—but they do see a roll of bills he flashes around. In the night they kill him for the money. In the morning, his wife arrives and reveals his identity, whereupon the mother and sister kill themselves.

The son unwittingly sets a deadly drama in motion, but fails to notify all the players of their roles. His mother and sister interpret him as a stranger. It is easier to rob and kill a stranger than a son and brother. Their interpretation of who he was (and was not) makes all the difference. In the same way, every interpretation of a situation can make a determinative difference in how we relate to what is occurring there.

Interpretation is a dialogical or reflexive act in which the relationship between self and other, self and world, is defined.

Is this an emergency?—has to do with the situation of the other. Does it fall to me to respond?—depends upon my interpretation of how to position myself toward that reality. A decision about how to react in a certain situation is an interpretation of myself, as well as of the situation. Self and situation are reflexively joined in the interpretive act.

Interpretation involves ascertaining the facts of a situation, evaluating their relationship to another (pressing them into a pattern), and figuring out their meaning and implication for oneself. Seeing suffering is not enough; it is quite possible to see suffering and interpret it as deserved. Jeff's early confrontations with suffering led him to reject those who suffered. But those confrontations were dramatic enough to force him to start thinking about the adequacy of his interpretation, and then to change his interpretation.

Well, you can't help but really notice the extreme poverty, especially in Mexico City. It was pretty hard not to see it. I think you're affected by it. I don't know that you have an immediate sympathetic kind of reaction. First of all you are sort of disgusted. Just like handicapped people. You consider these people abnormal, and they're sort of offensive to you, because it's just too different.

It really shakes you up and then after a while you begin thinking, why are these people like this? And you enter into discussion with other people's ideas—"They're just genetically inferior; they're stupid; they're lazy," whatever it is. The experiences were dramatic enough so that you had to rationalize them one way or another.

Every setting is interpreted, but not all interpretations evidence a positive moral stance.

The interviews did not focus on questions of moral justification, nor did we ask the participants to reflect aloud about their own norms or values. Moral categories and qualities are, nonetheless, much in evidence in the interviews. The interviews are moral interpretations of the human world.

There is some explicit use of moral language. "It was immoral to live that way; it wasn't fair; that just isn't good." Descriptions of how the participants reacted to some of the settings also reflect traditional moral language. "Somebody ought to do something about that; I just felt I had to act." There are scattered references to justice, equality, and fairness.

Beside these uses of recognizable moral language, there are other less obvious dimensions of moral interpretation. Descriptions can have moral force without using traditional normative language. A storyteller does not have to attach the label "unjust" if the tale clearly identifies manifestly unjust actions. In the context of an interview about how one became socially active, a sympathetic description of preventable suffering does not require labels like "unfair" to express its morally compelling quality. The drama of a description of slow starvation actually has more force than a statement like "starvation is bad." These descriptions are also de facto justifications of and invitations to involvement. They are not arguments in any formal philosophical sense; they are arguments in a human sense. They are explanations with the force of justification, descriptions with the force of moral argument.

The movement from sleeping to waking is also a shift—from disengagement with the world to engagement in it. Assertions like "it grabbed me; it tugged at my heart; it really made me angry" suggest that emotion is intertwined with perception and interpretation. "I find myself quickly deciding how do I feel about these issues. It's so quick that I say it's almost gut level—I don't even think about it a lot of times."

In *The Passions*, Robert Solomon articulates a perspective on the emotions that parallels the evidence in the interviews. Solomon points out that emotions are not just reactions; they are evaluations, judgments, and interpretations.[11] When a person witnesses an event, any sort of response—from averting one's eyes to peering intently, from apathy to anger—is an emotional judgment about the event.

Perception and interpretation only exist apart from emotion in the analytic treatments of textbooks. They co-exist in people. Thus, various assertions made earlier have suggested the emotional dimension. Emotion is a reaching out toward or avoidance of something. Our emotions are numb or attuned to the possibilities of engagement with situations. Emotions ignore or internalize what is encountered. In emotion we define not only the setting, but reflexively, who we are in our relationship to it—its meaning to us, and with that—our self-meaning. "Through our emotions we constitute and mythologize our world, projecting our values and passing judgments on ourselves and other people, our situations and the various 'intentional objects' in which we have invested our interests."[12]

Solomon points out that "many emotions have a distinctly moral edge to their judgments." . . . "Anger is not only a constitutive judgment of accusation and guilt; it is also an ideology which demands rectification and the balance of justice in the world."[13] (I would substitute the word "carries" or "co-exists with" for the word "is" in "it *is* an ideology," but otherwise find that his description fits the interviews.) Emotion constitutes the tenor, the intensity, of our attending-toward the world as a moral phenomenon. Leaning-toward might even be a better metaphor, for it connotes the positioning of our body, our whole selves, not just our minds, toward the world of people and nature.

Coming to awareness is a preliminary judgment about activation. Change in awareness involves the constitution or reconstitution of a moral horizon. Perception, interpretation, and emotion constitute the frames of our consciousness. Awareness that is good is comprised of accurate perception, adequate interpretation, and appropriate emotion.

—5—
THE
ACTIVATION
OF COMMITMENT

It is satisfying, perhaps beguiling, to become newly aware of the world's social and moral problems. Those made newly aware may believe they have arrived at a higher moral state now that they have seen the light. Other less enlightened people obviously have a narrow and ill-informed view of the world. Awareness without significant action is perhaps the most insidious liberal trap. Individuals may feel they are on top of the situation because they *understand* it. Kenneth Keniston calls the aware but uninvolved person a curdled idealist or a latent radical, one who lacks a "commitment to action and a sense of engagement with others who seek to change society."[1] The aware person has a sense of moral OK-ness without doing much to alleviate suffering or bring about justice in a troubled world.

The feeling of being one who knows may be satisfying, but it is not terribly helpful to those who suffer great injustice. Furthermore, it is a stunting of the human drive toward self-expression, the completion of thoughts in deeds. It also ignores the responsibility laid upon us by virtue of our participation in the human community. The community provides us with language, art, music, culture, and the opportunity for work and expression. These gifts need to be maintained and passed along in good condition—the gifts of love and life call for a gesture of response.

Many are concerned; few become involved. Social researchers have documented the large gap that exists between the ability to articulate adequate values and the willingness to act on them. What further steps beyond awareness go into the making of an activist? Researchers disagree partly because they study different kinds of activism. Kenneth Keniston studied Vietnam era peace activists. Perry London interviewed Christians who took personal risks to rescue Jews from Germany.[2] Some studied the reactions of people in concentration camps; others devised streetcorner experiments to determine the circumstances under which individuals will or will not help a person who seems to have a problem.[3] The differences between helping Jews in Nazi Germany and helping someone who falls down at a street corner are so great that it is little wonder that studies arrive at different conclusions about the causes of involvement.

An interview reports the first-hand experience of Pat, who held elective office in state government. "How did you happen to become socially active?" she was asked.

In my own life, let's see when it would have been. In 1950, for the first time I was spurred on to certain activities when I had a five-year-old son who wanted to go to kindergarten. At that time you had to pay to get into kindergarten, and not enough parents were willing to pay that nine dollars a month tuition for children to attend. Up at the school I ran into another mother. We stopped and talked about it, and we decided we'd just attack it head on.

So we went down to the old administration building, which was up on State and Commerce streets, to visit the school census in that district. We copied down the names, addresses, and phone numbers of every parent of a child five years old in the area of that particular school. When we got through, we went back home and got on the phone and we called them. And we had a kindergarten that year!

I think that is the sort of thing many people do. In fact, while I was looking back one day, that was the first time I remember getting out into it and saying "By gosh this needs to be done, and nobody's gonna do it if we don't." And we did. It sounds like a

small thing, and yet it required someone to go out and call up people and say, "Do you want your child to get used to school before really she has to start learning?"

From then on down through the years I guess joining the League of Women Voters was next. I joined the League of Women Voters in the early sixties and became very aware. And so I took action as a member of that group in many different ways. Sometimes I'd make a suggestion or recommendation, participating in group discussion: "We need to take a stand on this; we need to study this next year; this is a real problem"

After that . . . [She went on to talk about a job and other activities that raised her awareness and in which she acquired political skills. She also described how a woman friend had been discriminated against.]

Anyway, I got into the woman's movement then because it dawned on me this was a terrible injustice. When someone you know gets hurt or is affected by something, you become strongly aware of it. Now here's my son not being able to go to kindergarten, my friend being fired. And as a result of that, I guess I got interested in the Equal Rights Amendment in Michigan, and all my activities. And that's sort of how I got into politics.

I became more of an activist all the time in terms of thinking there was a lack of representation. I never ran for anything in my life until I ran for state office. By that time I got involved in organizing or founding a women's political caucus. I got a lot of good out of that. That work there was valuable. Certainly women are politically involved. They are the ones that carry the burden of the campaign on their shoulders. I found out you put your body where your mouth is. My first reaction to the suggestion that I run for office was "Me? Not me!" That was in the fall of 1974. Then I ran in 1975. That came about as a result of the way I got involved.

I found myself eagerly involved because I got a little involved right down the line, so you know one thing leads to another, and that wasn't the only reason I ran. While in the League of Women Voters, I had thought for a long time that people in this area had not been properly represented, needed better representation. And I'd do my best to replace at least one of the representatives. Oh yes, I left something out. I should have said that I joined the

National Organization for Women in 1970, about the time this friend was fired. And they were very helpful. I'm sorry; I didn't mean to leave them out.

Personal Effectiveness

One factor essential to the making of an activist is a sense of personal effectiveness. Most latent radicals, Keniston suggests, "are never activated because they assume that effective action is (1) essential but (2) impossible." Therefore, why waste time? The assumption that the task is impossible can be overcome when activists believe that their actions do have an effect, or decide that success is not important—that something must be done even though there is no assurance that it will change anything.[4] "I couldn't just sit and watch it. Even spinning one's wheels makes one feel as if one is doing something, if the alternative is doing nothing," said one of our participants. Thus, many people work to bring about changes but are not at all sure that the desired effect will be achieved. For example, many work to prevent nuclear war with the sure knowledge that such a war could easily occur before the long-term effects of their peacemaking are felt. But there is a sense of the intrinsic magnitude of the problem that compels them to respond, even though they have no control over or assurance about the outcome. This sense of urgency is crucial for social action.

Pat's whole story can be seen as an extended presentation of how she acquired the sense of personal effectiveness that enabled her to move from homemaker to officeholder. "We had a kindergarten that year!" she says triumphantly. And then again a few sentences later, "We did it!" Nothing fortifies the identity of an activist like success in changing something—almost anything, for that matter. The we-did-it sums up and fixes in the consciousness a symbolic moment that prepares a person for later, perhaps more adventuresome engagements. After the kindergarten episode, she worked in an agency where she met many public figures and learned the political ropes. Her participation in the League of Women Voters, the National Organization for Women, and a Women's Political Caucus helped her acquire the confidence and skill required for a legislative race.

The kindergarten episode seems rather insignificant. Is this what is meant by social action? Pat herself seems a bit embarrassed, "It seems like such a small thing." But as a first act, it marks a beginning point in the evolution of her politization. Other people have also found their involvement gradually deepening through an escalating series of commitments. As Rob said:

My wife got me to join the ACLU with her. Then you begin running into some cases. Then you are asked to do some work on them. Then you begin to meet some people who are interested in similar items. Then you might serve on a committee or give a speech some place. So you gradually work into something.

Perry London recounts the story of a German who devoted his personal fortune and four years of his life to save about two hundred Jews from the Nazis. The man agreed at first just to take the husband of his secretary. " 'I started with one person, then six people, from there to 50, then 100.' "[5]

By way of contrast, Michelle's initiation was somewhat more abrupt. She had been terribly afraid of speaking in public. "If my name were called on attendance my heart would start beating faster as my name approached." She went along with a friend to pick up some new federal welfare guidelines. That night she studied them. The next day she went along with her friend to a meeting of welfare mothers in a housing project. Suddenly her friend introduced her and said Michelle would explain the HEW guidelines and help them fill out the forms. "There was no time for protest; there was nothing to do but stand up and tell them what I had read. Drop me into the water and I just had to swim. So I did it. When I finished my friend said I did very well, and I was thrilled to death. I was somewhat intoxicated by my first success." As always, nothing succeeds like success.

Many disparate things lead a person to act or not act. *Situational factors*—such as immediate access to the problem and convenience—can exert a determinative influence on whether one will act on a specific occasion. Behavioral studies suggest that a person who is less encumbered is more likely to respond to an emergency, than someone who is more encumbered.[6] One of the most frequently cited behavioral studies is called the good Samaritan experiment.[7]

Forty Princeton seminarians were asked to give a short talk—some on the parable of the good Samaritan, others to compare ministry with different occupations. Each was asked to go to another building to deliver the talk. On the way to their appointment each seminarian encountered a man "sitting slumped in a doorway, head down, eyes closed, not moving. As the subject went by, the victim coughed twice and groaned, keeping his head down."[8] The primary question was whether those who were to speak on the good Samaritan, who presumably had helping someone in need on their mind would be more likely to help a distressed person by their wayside than students whose topic was more neutral.

A second variable introduced into the research was a degree of hurriedness. One group of students was told to hurry right over; the program was running late. A second group was simply told to be prompt. A third group was told they had a few minutes until they were due at the other building, but that they should head on over. The research found that it did not matter which talk a seminarian was giving, but that it mattered very much whether the seminarian was in a hurry.

A person in a hurry was unlikely to stop, whereas a person who had extra time was more likely to stop and help. Darley and Batson noted that "Indeed, on several occasions, a seminary student going to give his talk on the parable of the Good Samaritan literally stepped over the victim as he hurried on his way!"[9]

They had, after all, framed the whole event in their consciousness in a way that led them not to notice such things as a person slumped in a doorway. Or, it could be pointed out that that part of urban survival means learning to mind your own business. Whatever truth there is in these explanations, the fact remains that those in less of a hurry did stop more often. Degree of hurriedness is one of the many situational factors that may make the difference between response and nonresponse.

Because situational factors influence people's response, the good society cannot be built through producing good people one at a time—by a strategy of inculcating good values, thoughts, ideals, or even individual moral conversions. The society itself becomes a situation that must be structured in ways leading people to act in a moral manner. This point is similar to that made in the midst of the civil rights movement of the 1960s (and at a more general level by Aristotle)—social problems will not be eradicated by individual moral conversions. A social order in which policy, structure, and ethos militate against a problem at every level is required before the problem can be eliminated. Likewise, it is necessary to fashion a society with characteristics that facilitate social involvement—with an ethos of responsiveness and responsibility, rather than of atomistic individuality and irresponsibility. In any case, this first aspect of the can-do experience emphasizes such accidental features of a situation as convenience and hurriedness.

Another ingredient in the can-do experience is the *acquisition of knowledge or techniques* required to perform tasks. "I didn't know how to respond; I felt helpless; I didn't know where to begin." Behavioral studies suggest that in emergency situations, bystanders routinely defer to other bystanders who seem to have more knowledge about what to do, such as medical personnel in medical emergencies.[10]

Alfred Schutz's description of the I-can-do-it-again experience highlights a person's sense of confidence—because of a prior experience, one has the knowledge or techniques to do something.[11] Berger and Luckmann refer to this how-to knowledge as recipe or cookbook knowledge. One who has the knowledge is equipped to carry out a routine performance. If you know how, it may be easy—if you don't, it is one big mystery. "Once you take the first step, it's a little easier." A pedagogy for activism would have to include knowledge of the routine performances required in action contexts.

At a more profound level, the I-can-do experience has to do with *power, embodiment and identity:* I (identity) + can (ability, power) + do (effect by means of my body).

It is difficult to overestimate the foundational character of our acts of doing (as distinguished from thinking acts or feeling acts). Our bodies are the primary agent through which we gear into the world, the medium through which wanting and willing are actualized. The body "is that by means of which my 'I can' is most immediately actualized: wanting to raise the glass to my lips, this volition is immediately actualized by my body."[12]

From our very first days, can-do is connected with successful bodily performances. Parents lavish praise on such performances; the tiniest infant learns to feel good when she can-do, and bad when she cannot. "Our baby can smile, hold up her head, crawl, talk, walk, jump, climb, hit a home run." Growth means mastery of ever larger regions of experience. If a person becomes old, ill, or handicapped, I-can-no-longer-do reaches deeply into and threatens one's identity. When one cannot-do the frustration is enormous. Doing acts are primary vehicles of human self-expression. I must "unfold my existence by means of my body."[13]

The body metaphors of activation were somewhat different than those of awareness metaphors. Whereas awareness metaphors are more passive, emphasizing something happening to oneself, activation metaphors tend to be more active. Pat uses three of the most common: (1) "We'd just attack head on," (2) "We need to take a stand," and (3) "You put your body where your mouth is." One thread common to all three metaphors is the sense of engaging one's body in the activities of the social world. Thought, the activity of mind, does not realize the full, or even the central meaning of political action. To attack head on is to charge forward. To take a stand or to put one's body on the line is to fortify oneself for attack, assert oneself—to risk one's precious self. To put your body where your mouth is suggests that talk is cheap, that it is time for words and deeds to become congruent—time to risk your body, not just your words. "It was time to stop [just] feeling and start doing."

This can-do goes beyond matters of convenience or recipe knowledge to personal empowerment. Personal empowerment may be specific or general—"I have this power to do this activity" or "I am the sort of person who is powerful and can do things." The first statement asserts self-confidence in a particular region of experience; the second avers that a powerful person can do many/most things. Coleen: "You have to become someone and be powerful in order to bring about some sort of change."

This can-do experience helps explain two of the responses that for a long time confused me. Why did blacks make such a point of their going to college as an important step in their becoming politically active? And what was the connection between a failed marriage and activation? Both cases had to do with overcoming the past—especially fear—and acquiring a sense of personal power.

Karen articulated the themes of knowledge, fear, and power in relation to her marriage and her first steps in political involvement. She had joined a Women's Political Caucus. "We organized the first of July." The leader of the group was ready to move.

She comes in one day in August and says, "Well, I think our first project will be the Metro City banks." And here she is, all four feet ten of her, and she says we're going to call ninety Metro City banks. She was just crazy enough to take on these things, and none of the rest of us would have had the nerve to do it. It was mind-blowing. Our self-image was that we were just dumb women. I know I was bright in a way, and yet I was terribly intimidated by the establishment world.

She had been down at the Federal Building researching how you file charges, what the laws were, how all this stuff works. She was a brilliant woman. Then she came back and explained it to me. "This is what you do. We're going to call these banks on the phone and ask them these questions." Looking back I realize she was just as shaken as I was. But she wasn't about to be deterred by that. Most of us would never have had the nerve to make that kind of step.

Actually, she didn't want to call these banks either. She had me do it. But she says, "All right now, you call these banks and you ask them blah, blah, blah, and then call me back and tell me what they say." The act of having to pick up that phone and call the Federal National Bank, now that was really scary. I'm going to call Federal National Bank and ask a vice-president in charge of personnel? I mean I was scared to move.

The Federal National Bank was this enormous building downtown with these important people. Even though in part of my head I knew they weren't any brighter than I was, still I was terribly intimidated as most of us are by big institutions. I was going to call the Federal National Bank and ask them out of the blue? Who am I to ask them, "What is your pregnancy policy?" and "How many women officers do you have?" Doing that was a really difficult thing—picking up the phone and calling and saying, "I want to speak to so and so." And you get them on the phone and you say, "I'm so and so, could you tell me, blah, blah." Well, once we started, once you take the first step, then it gets a little easier.

Maybe it even got to be sort of fun to see what kind of games you play, because Federal National was particularly evasive; they played all kinds of games. You had to try to figure out how to outsmart them to get the information out of them. It got to be interesting, though it was still scary the whole time.

Once we had gotten the information together, we had to have the first press conference to announce that we had done this study and were filing charges with the Treasury Department against thirty Metro City banks, which was really big news in Metro City at that time. That just wasn't done. And Roy asked me not to go to the press conference because he did business with all those banks. And chicken that I was, I didn't go.

But others went, and it was still terribly exciting. Here we were. Who were we? Nobody, you know. And here we were filing charges against these banks, and we were on TV, and we were in the headlines. Suddenly we were reflected back to ourselves in a completely different light. We were frightening people. Look what we'd done to the banks. It had unnerved the banks. They were scared ———! Just these little old women filed charges, and they were scared to death. They were most upset—the reaction was very strong. So we went on from there. I took over and headed up the rest of the studies and did all the press conferences and so forth. That transformation of suddenly seeing yourself reflected back from a completely different light from anything you were used to is mind-blowing.

I discovered I was an excellent public speaker. I was loving all the excitement of the women's movement. And I was good at doing a lot of these things, and really and thoroughly enjoyed it. I had not been aware before of how invisible I was. But suddenly I realized what it is to be a man, what it is to say something and have people listen seriously to what you're saying. It was a new phenomenon for me.

Several months of that did a lot for changing my self-confidence and image of myself and how I saw myself reflected in other people's eyes as an important person, someone worth listening to, someone who can do things, someone you respect. So that was a very valuable experience for me, those two years. By the time it was over with, I had gotten a lot of things out of my system and a lot of things behind me. Something about my own attitude toward myself was an accomplished fact by the time it was over with.

Meanwhile, Roy and I had unsuccessfully been trying to work through our marital problems. Finally, I said, "It's not working; let's forget it." When I had first broached the subject of having to change this or leave two or three years before that, it scared the ———— out of me to think about getting a divorce, really scared me to my roots because I hadn't been on my own—all that basic insecurity. I had been married since eighteen and been dependent in important ways on a superior figure. The idea that I could step out and shake that off was so frightening at first, that I could hardly handle it. But by the time I did—I had been pulling this all together for two years—by then it was no problem to say, "It's over and this isn't working and it's time to split." It was a very easy step to make by that time.

Q: How intensively can you remember any of these things that were meaningful or important to you?

Let's see if I can focus on some things. I told you about reading *The Feminine Mystique* and the realization that was crystallizing things that had been running along under my surface for years. It came to a head that spring, I finally was able to act on these things. My husband did a lot of traveling. We were at a resort where he was doing business. I was sitting in a townhouse reading magazines for the day while he worked. They had these old magazines around with a lot of women's lib stuff, just like *Redbook* and stuff that just happened to have some women's lib articles. I had been for months reading this stuff, and that day I sat down and immediately grabbed whatever sounded like women's lib and was reading through it, and spent the day mulling over this stuff and was feeling this resentment because Roy was off working and I was stuck here—a sort of the kept-in wife. And I realized that day that I had to act on this which was a gut wrench because acting on it was really scary. It meant confronting Roy with all that he represented of power and parental figures. I had been reading for maybe five or six months. I finally had it together enough that I could now do something with it; I was going to have to do it eventually. And that day, finally, it had to be done.

It was a beautiful night. We went out to dinner. I'll never forget the scene; it was such a highlight of my life. Always before when we discussed these things, I would end up in tears. Well, tonight I had to be in control enough to say, "This is the way it is," without dissolving. So we got to dinner at this lovely restaurant, marvelous food. We sit down at the table and I start out. And immediately it's this great thing, I am in control. I know what I'm saying, and I believe in it, and Roy goes pale. He doesn't eat a bit of his dinner.

It's not so much his impotence in the situation, but the feeling that I'm not impotent. Here he is in the position I've been in for years, and I'm in control, and it's such a marvelous feeling. I just lay it out for him—it becomes easier and easier as we go along when I see that he doesn't know how to handle the situation. I am so in control of the materials by now. I mean, I can argue anything because I've read so much by that point I've got it all together. I just laid out for him why I was unhappy with the marriage and why this was not fair and wasn't right, and we had to change it, or the marriage should come to an end. I was so cool and calm; it was just marvelous; it was one of those golden moments. That was when we began aggressively working with the marriage, or at least I began aggressively working with the marriage. He did as best he could. At the time it was a great liberation from where I had been.

In order to get started in political involvement, one first has to overcome inertia and fear, has to have a sense of personal power. Al describes his first civil rights march as "the beginning of my bravery." Ben describes his first time to picket as involving "excitement, fear, a rebirth. I wanted to. I wanted to. I was frightened. That's when I finally developed guts." Or, as Judy challenged LuAnn, "Imagine you are Joan of Arc or something, but get over here and do this press conference."

Alfred Schutz describes the immediate circle around our bodies as a manipulatory zone, "the region open to my immediate interference which I can modify either directly by movements of my body or with . . . tools." Objects in this zone are experienced as intensively real; they have substance; they resist when I touch them. This zone represents the "kernel of the reality of the life-world."[14] It is the primary zone of our embodied can-do experience.

Since the manipulatory zone, the world of working, is experienced as the paramount reality, things removed by degrees from that zone not only seem less real, they are less under our control. We can't reach out and move them around, and when we push, they are less likely to give. The farther out the zone of reality and the greater the magnitude of the problem there, the more helpless we feel about doing anything to change the situation. Or, we assume that somebody else will do it. News media reports of the activities of politicians and other public leaders give us the feeling that somebody powerful is acting on the problems, or at least trying to. If the president can't get his way, what hope is there that we can affect things? We experience ourselves as the audience watching someone else's play, not the actors. It is only in the more immediate world of home and work that we have more sense of personal effectiveness, of ability to influence events.

I recently called a community organizer in another city to ask him a question about his involvement. "We've been really busy," he volunteered. "We spend the morning conferring with our senator. It gives you a powerful feeling to be strategizing with a U.S. Senator." Unless we are able to sustain motivation solely by commitment to a compelling vision, we need a sense of effectiveness, feeling we have influenced events or the system in some way. "There was first anxiety and then the amazing discovery that I could actually do something to help another human being." A few we-did-it experiences, a few victories at a symbolic level, empower and sustain a person in the action world for a long period of time. Winning is fun, but having an effect on the system brings a lasting sense of satisfaction—lasting because the benefits just keep rolling on once they have been built into the structure, and because they affect so many people. Changing the system is a way of loving, not one, but many neighbors as oneself. It is participating in the creating of a more just and humane world, redirecting the ongoing stream of history in however small a way.

An opposite of the can-do experience is the reaction "There was nothing we could do to stop the war. We were seeing the need, but I can't stop the war." A perception that one cannot-do leads to inaction. Such a perception is, of course, partly accurate. The average citizen is well aware that alone he or she cannot stop a war. But in seeing the immensity of its evil, we want to. It is necessary to change our understanding of our relation to such events. We can *affect*, but not alone *effect*. Dom Helder Camara said in the movie *Excuse Me, America* that when we dream alone, it is a dream—when we dream together, it is the beginning of reality.

In addition to empowerment there is a sense of *at-homeness* in the world of political action. It is one thing to know I can-do, even that I have-done; it is another to know that "I am at home doing" it.

The potential activist needs to establish a degree of familiarity, of comfort, of "being at home" in the world of political action. People speak of "getting out into it." The move from noninvolvement to involvement requires a leap from familiar to unfamiliar zones of reality. A pedagogy for social action would get people into the arenas where the action occurs so that they can overcome their fears, become at home with the world of involvement, and get some feeling that their activities contribute to a larger whole.

Personal Responsibility

A person also must develop a sense of personal responsibility to intervene—"must come to feel personally responsible for effecting change."[15] Responsibility literally means "the liability for making a response." The word connotes "ought to do," and is clearly distinguishable from the foregoing can-do.

The word "responsibility" first appeared in the context of the French and American revolutions. The *Oxford English Dictionary* lists Alexander Hamilton as the first to use the word in English (in 1787). That same year *responsabilité* appeared in French. The origins of the word are rooted in political discourse.[16] In subsequent philosophical treatments, the dominant meaning has remained on the ought-to side; a responsible person is one who does what ought to be done, who fulfills the liability for response.

In the interviews "I felt I must do something" and "If I don't do it, nobody will" express a sense of personal responsibility to act. Phrases like these express more of an inner urgency to act than a response to external authority. There is a sense of ought-to, but that sense arises from within rather than in response to orders from some external authority or even from obligations imposed by legal contracts. "I felt I ought to do something" may be an external "you ought to do something" that has been internalized. Even if that is the case (and I am not convinced that it is) there is still a sense of ownness, voluntariness, or "I really want to" about it. It rises from within in direct response to a setting, rather than being laid on as an obligation from some outside source.

This inner sense of responsibility is more powerful than obedient response to authority or response to legal contract. (There may be a kind of implicit contract here—because you are human I owe it to you.) The power of "I must do something about it" resides precisely in the fact that one wants to or feels inwardly motivated to act. This action is self-initiated rather than compliance to some external authority or standard.

> Without our being, at least by disposition, responsive to the call of duty in terms of feeling, the most cogent demonstration of its right, even when compelling theoretical assent, would be powerless to make it a motivating force. . . . In any case, the gap between abstract validation and concrete motivation must be bridged by the arc of sentiment, which alone can sway the will.[17]

In Pat's case, as in many spontaneous acts, there is an "it falls to me to do it," or an "it is mine to do." There is a personalizing of responsibility, not just that somebody ought to do something, but "I am the somebody." This personalizing of responsibility may be occasioned several ways. One root is self-interest: "It was my son who needed a kindergarten class." Pat had a personal stake—something to gain—from the outcome; it was in her self-interest to act. It did not require any altruism.

Related to personal stake is a sense of personal connection with the person who has the problem: "It was my friend who had been fired," said Pat. This sense of personal connection can rise out of something as ephemeral as proximity. We have more sense of personal connection with a neighbor or a loved one than a stranger or foreigner. We even may have more sense of connection to a stranger close at hand than one far away.

The Milgram experiment suggests a correlation between proximity and willingness to administer increasing doses of electric shock to an innocent victim.[18] When the subject could not see the victim, the subject was more likely to administer ever higher voltage shocks. When the victim could be seen, compliance to an order to administer the shock dropped off. And when the subject had to force the victim's hand onto a plate to complete the circuit, compliance was lowest. A sense of personal responsibility is positively correlated with the extent of a connection with the victim. This is even more dramatically true in cases where an emotional relationship exists between sufferer and potential deliverer.

Some people have an extended sense of personal connection. They feel connected with other people, even though the connection seems rather tenuous to an observer. Dorothy Day describes how Upton Sinclair in *The Jungle* helped her make a personal connection with poor people, which led to her involvement.

> Though my only experience of the destitute was in books, the very fact that *The Jungle* was about Chicago where I lived, whose streets I walked, made me feel that from then on my life was to be linked to theirs, their interests were to be mine; I had received a call, a vocation, a direction to my life.[19]

Day and others have a capacity that enables them to internalize the texture and meaning of other persons' lives. This sense of connection in its largest expression is "Because I am human and she is human, I have a connection with her, a responsibility toward her."

One of the chief expressions of this personalizing of responsibility was "If I don't do it, nobody will"—"By gosh this needs to be done, and nobody's going to do it if we don't." Marjorie explained that she called a Student Nonviolent

Coordinating Committee meeting on campus in the 1960s because "I thought it was important. Ain't nobody else was calling a meeting." There is a sense of urgency that something happen, and the growing awareness that "I am the somebody" who is going to do it. Responsibility is not diffused; it is mine!

Behavioral studies suggest that when a person is in a crowd and an emergency occurs, that person is less likely to respond than if alone.[20] The person standing in a crowd knows that somebody else might stop and help; responsibility is diffused. But when alone in a developing emergency, either that person does something or nobody will. Unfortunately, most of us in a mass society experience ourselves as living in the midst of a very big crowd indeed.

The flip side of "If I don't do it nobody will" is "Why me, O Lord," the feeling that one has been singled out in a particular kind of way for some misfortune. David wryly commented that in the labors of his social involvements, he often felt exasperated, "Why me, O Lord, . . . why am I called to the burden of this energy-consuming work?"

Alongside of have-the-ability-to, can-influence, and mine-to-do, is a sense of calling or must-do. The I-must-do experience is perhaps the most important element in personal responsibility and the activation process generally. Many stories of personal heroism and foolishness arise out of this impulsive sort of response—the young man who cannot swim but who leaps into the water to save his drowning brother. Some people feel driven into political action, even though they do not have the vaguest idea of what to do or how to do it. Their sense of must-do drives them into social action arenas where they acquire can-do, or even act blindly without it.

By itself, training in techniques will never produce an activist. Activation does not depend primarily on adequate training (though to remain an activist over a period of time, one must acquire can-do) or even a fully developed sense of personal power. Many people feel that they are driven to act, and it is only once in the midst of the action that they learn how to negotiate the system and become effective political actors. Pat spoke of being "spurred on" to action. This metaphor catches the typical sense of drivenness that characterizes the must-do feeling; it is a welling up of willing. It is an "ought" experienced as inner imperative, obligation experienced as seduction. It is an "act of volitional proposing."[21]

The situation of the other person incites a claim so powerful that we feel compelled to respond. "This has to stop." "I had to take a stand." "I've got to do something about it." "I was propelled into it." "There is something I have to do. As a concerned individual I have to go back to Guatemala."

Marjorie is a black woman with a national reputation. Her memories recapture the urgency of the sixties.

I was part of a generation that began to question. I remember being shocked when the four girls in Birmingham were killed. I was visiting there. And people thought, "This has to stop!"

My thought was the same as anybody else's—that if you're going to bomb somebody's churches, then you'll have to pay for that. It is one thing if you want to bomb people when they come out of church. That's fair; that's war. But if you're going to bomb churches and Sunday schools with little girls in them, then you're going to pay. And of course they did. So that the riots in the cities weren't a shock to me. I had no difficulty at all supporting it. Of course you burn a city down! That's the least that you do. Of course you shoot back. Who wants to watch your children get blown up on Sunday?

Of course you do that! Of course you defend yourself! Malcolm X was no shock to us. Of course you take whatever steps are necessary to take, because it is insanity to allow that to go on. I wouldn't have been surprised if I had ended up with a rifle in my hand. That wouldn't have surprised me in the sixties because it was an unacceptable situation.

It was a totally unacceptable situation by any standards. So whatever has to stop that, let's do it. Hopefully you won't get hurt, or you won't hurt somebody else, but it has to stop!

If my generation would let that go on then, when would it stop? We really did quite a bit to bring America into the twentieth century, because it was really archaic. White boys thought they had a right to come into the dormitory and shoot, or whatever they felt like doing. We were making animals out of white people. If we refused to stand and fight for ourselves, then they were going to continue to be animals. And it was amazing how their behavior turned around the minute people started

saying, "Hey, look. If you put your hands on me, that's gonna be the last time those hands touch anything." All of a sudden they found out they didn't want to beat you so much. You have to stop people from being animals, or they will continue to be animals.

Decision

A chief difference between the coming to awareness and activation of commitment experiences is that the former is received more passively, whereas the latter has more the character of motion and decision, as in "It got me moving," and "I decided that it just had to stop." This is as expected, for the very nature of social action is activity—doing—putting one's body in motion in order to accomplish something.

A November 1971 article describes the conversion of Daniel Ellsberg from supporting to opposing the United States' involvement in Vietnam. The article describes both awareness and activation. "The conversion was as gradual as it was absolute, and Ellsberg speaks of a time 'when I walked through American society looking for a place to stand.' " Ellsberg was impressed by Randy Kehler, a draft resister who was sent to jail for his beliefs. "The final blow came that fall when Ellsberg read a newspaper account of the case of the Green Berets who had been charged with the murder of a double agent; . . . On the day of the Green Beret story, Ellsberg decided 'to stop lying.' "[22]

The decision to do something is typically not arrived at by a process of gradually sorting through the logical options and then making a conscious choice among them. Decision in these cases is more a spontaneous commitment than a rational judgment. There are in the interviews only two clear exceptions to this—two persons who indicate that their social involvement was predicated upon careful rational thought. The social action of both consists largely of things like speaking to community groups and writing letters to the editor. In contrast, the decision to become involved frequently comes in a highly charged moment—a triggering incident in which one is overwhelmed by a sense of "must do." It is experienced as arriving at the will to act, rather than a reflective choice among deeds. Decision precedes conscious reflection.

A study of the decision-making of twenty kidney transplant donors followed the donors though a long process of screening, testing, and briefing in which they were informed about the risks. Only at the end of this process were the potential donors asked to decide whether they would permit the removal of one of their kidneys. Such a procedure is painful and not without its own risks. Under those circumstances people might reflect rather carefully before making a final decision. Instead, "It appeared that not one of the donors weighed the alternatives and decided rationally." Most said that they had "made their decision immediately when the subject of the kidney transplant was first mentioned over the telephone 'in a split second,' 'instantaneously,' 'right away.' "[23] The fact that these decisions flow so spontaneously from established frames of reference makes these frames all the more important.

Margaret Sanger recorded the events that changed her from nurse to champion of birth control. Day after day she had been confronted with the agony of poor women whose problems stemmed from "destitution linked with excessive childbearing."

> These were not merely "unfortunate conditions among the poor" such as we read about. I knew the women personally. They were living, breathing, human beings, with hopes, fears, and aspirations like my own, yet their weary, misshapen bodies . . . were destined to be thrown on the scrap heap before they were thirty-five . . . . My own cozy and comfortable family existence was becoming a reproach to me.[24]

She goes on to describe Mrs. Sachs, a twenty-eight-year-old woman who had contracted septicemia as a result of a self-induced abortion. Mrs. Sachs narrowly survived with the help of Sanger, the doctor, and her husband. The doctor warned her that one more time might prove fatal. She begged the doctor to tell her what she could do to prevent pregnancy. The doctor said, "Tell Jake to sleep on the roof." Mrs. Sachs turned to Margaret Sanger and pleaded, "Please tell me the secret, and I'll never breathe it to a soul. *Please!*"[25]

Sanger was haunted by the request but did nothing. Three months later Jake called. Mrs. Sachs had again become pregnant, aborted, and had an infection.

For a wild moment I thought of sending someone else, but actually, of course, I hurried into my uniform, caught up my bag, and started out. All the way I longed for a subway wreck, an explosion, anything to keep me from having to enter that home again. But nothing happened, even to delay me. I turned into the dingy doorway and climbed the familiar stairs once more. The children were there, young little things.

Mrs. Sachs was in a coma and died within ten minutes. I folded her still hands across her breast, remembering how they had pleaded with me, begging so humbly for the knowledge which was her right. I drew a sheet over her pallid face. Jake was sobbing, running his hands through his hair and pulling it out like an insane person. Over and over again he wailed, "My God! My God! My God!"[26]

Sanger left, and then walked the streets. After she arrived home, she stared out the window and imagined all the individual pains and grief that were occurring there—many of which she had witnessed on previous occasions.

The scenes piled one upon another on another. I could bear it no longer.

As I stood there the darkness faded. The sun came up and threw its reflection over the house tops. It was the dawn of a new day in my life also. The doubt and questioning, the experimenting and trying, were now to be put behind me. I knew I could not go back merely to keeping people alive.

I went to bed, knowing that no matter what it might cost, I was finished with palliatives and superficial cures; I was resolved to seek out the root of evil, to do something to change the destiny of mothers whose miseries were vast as the sky.[27]

The next line in her book begins a new chapter. "How were mothers to be saved?" This excerpt from her autobiography evidences the same sort of metaphors singled out for treatment earlier. Scene piled upon scene until a tipping point or a breakthrough occurred. The change was the dawn of a new day in her life. It was occasioned by a personal confrontation with intense human suffering. Suddenly she felt that she just had to do something, just had to respond. But she did not have the slightest idea what it was that she should or could do. Her inner sense of must-do drove her to seek the how-to's.

Sanger's decision to move toward systemic change, to get at

the root of the problem provides the crucial differentiation between social welfare and social action. Those who become activists are moved to address problems at the level of the structure of a society, and not just one at a time as such problems cross their path.

—6—
MORAL
CONVICTION

Awareness and activation are often triggered by a discovery of the contrast between two disjunctive realities. If being poor is the norm, the poor may not notice their poverty. They know they suffer, but there are no rich people with which to compare themselves. Anne: "Coming from a small town and then arriving in a large metropolitan city, I could see enormous gaps in income for the first time. I realized that some people had an awful lot more in the way of material goods than others. And I could see very sharp differences between groups." Jim: "And then all of a sudden you find out there are people that live better."

A graphic example of the way contrasts generate awareness and activation appears in Carl's comments. Carl describes himself as a black activist, a militant, and yet a statesman. He has, as his parents before him, a long history of working for racial equality.

I suppose that I would have a number of experiences that I could remember that awakened my social consciousness. Probably the first experience that I remember as a black boy in a desegregated neighborhood and school was when my best girl friend in the second grade refused to invite me to her birthday party, largely because her parents thought I was getting too big.

I had gone to the birthday parties in the kindergarten, the first grade, but in the second and third grade I wasn't invited.

She was a white girl. When we would play farmer in the dell, she was always the one that I would choose for the farmer's wife—a very beautiful girl. But this incident was really when I first realized what the brainwashing technique of being "colored" was. And I began through a period of years really to assess that. But that moment was my first shock of realizing that I was labeled as "colored," which means inferior. There was nothing inherent in my ability. I was always at the head of my class. I was one of the best athletes in the school teams. But I realized that there was nothing inherent in me. It was something society was imposing upon me that I was "colored."

Carl went on to talk about not being able to buy a banana split because the store didn't have plastic dishes to put them on, about how paper routes were the stepping stones for junior executives in his town and thus not available to blacks, about how the white community looked down upon the black minister and black lawyer "as a joke," about how his brother dated a very fair black girl and because the "local police mistook her for a white, they were evicted from the movie theater."

I remember a man who came to our town and impressed me considerably. He was only there for a short time, but he was a person who somehow instilled in us in that short period of time, that if we didn't speak up for our own rights nobody else would. This is the first time it occurred to me. I was about thirteen.

[A few years later, Carl was denied a college scholarship.] That decision was made between me and a blond-haired white boy that was two inches taller than I was. We had the same grade point average. We were both in extracurricular things. The thing that made it so pronounced was that I tried out for the same play and the same part. The part was for a tall butler and he got the part—with black make-up paint—and he was less than two inches taller than I was. The women's association granted the scholarship, and he got the scholarship and I didn't, and I determined right then that I was going to go to college. I worked nights; I waited tables, and I did all kinds of odd jobs and saved my money, because my parents weren't able to give me anything to help me through college. I was determined I was going to go to college just for that very reason. He really got that scholarship because he was white and I was black. And I knew it!

When I was in college, I was president of the college NAACP. I worked with the Congress of Racial Equality when it first came into being. I think one of the greatest coaches of all times was at that college, and I remember I went out for the team and he called me aside and said, "You know . . . ah . . . they say that Negroes sweat and they have an odor and . . . ah . . . ." And when he saw that didn't take, he said, "Well, ah . . . really, we haven't integrated our team here, but I understand you're good at some other sport. Why don't you go out and break in through that first?"

And when that argument didn't prevail, he said, "I'll tell you what. I can't keep you from coming out, but what I do is I usually use a winning combination and if you would make the first team and we went to play in the conference, I couldn't use you and it would upset my whole system of playing. So I would just say that I don't think that you should check out a suit."

To see him a few years later coach the U.S. Olympic team and come back, certainly a transformed converted man, and relate how proud he was to be an American when he saw a black boy put the U.S. on top when the points were close. And they played the "Star Spangled Banner" as this black boy stood on this podium glistening in sweat. How proud he was to be with this kind of a nation.

Birthday parties, a role in the school play, a missed scholarship, and exclusion from the team provided experiences that led to awareness and activation. The person who came to town and said "that if we didn't speak up for our own rights, nobody else would," played an important role. When Carl lost the scholarship, he "determined right then that I was going to go to college."

These several experiences were occasioned or heightened by contrasts or comparisons. Carl was invited to the birthday party for several years, then was not invited. The white boy was two inches taller but played a role in blackface. The coach who at one point worried about black odors, later bragged how proud he was to be an American when a black player won the winning points, and then "stood on this podium glistening in sweat." The discrimination against Carl was made all the more dramatic by the juxtaposition of these discordant realities. Jean: "My feminism grew out of an awareness that it was right for some people but not for others." Christi: "The street itself was in very poor condition, whereas the street in front of my house was in good shape."

Comparisons contain two poles, which could be called the "comparend" and the "comparee." The comparend is the standard, reference point, or base line against which the comparee is judged. If a person notes that one building is taller than another, one of the buildings has functioned as a standard (comparend) against which the other was described. We could say either "Building X is taller," or "Building Y is shorter." Objectively it comes to the same thing; subjectively there is a subtle difference. One building has become the reality worth noticing (taller) or the base line (shorter) against which the other is judged taller—taller than the short one.

When a person makes a moral decision, there are certain reference points to ground the judgment. I hand the bank teller a check for $100.60. He counts out $160. I think (in quick succession), "Wasn't the check for $100.60? He gave me too much. I could really use that money. Could I get away with it? Probably not. But then, who would know? It's not my fault he made a mistake. I can take the money and run. No, I'm not the sort of person who does things like that." The issue is decided when he notices my hesitation, takes the money back, looks again at the check, and counts out $100.60. My internal dialogue is a conversation with certain reference points—standards of fact and fairness, judgments pragmatic and normative, even a negotiation with my identity.

Parts of ourselves converse with other parts of ourselves—with norms, values, prior experiences, internalized voices. We juxtapose discordant facts and feelings, seek to put matters in a proper focus, search for a sensible way to resolve the issue at hand. Certain items become standards (comparends) against which others are judged. If the metaphor "dialogue" describes this process of decision making, some voices are louder than others. In moral decision making, the loud voices function as operative norms to the other voices.

One task of the discipline of ethics is to lift such standards up for examination at a conscious and intelligent level, rather than just allow them to shove us around. Though spontaneous remarks in autobiographical interviews are not as fully reflective as classroom ethics, this may not be the great loss that it at first seems to be. The interviews present actual (not just hypothetical) instances in which moral insight was attained (not just talked about). They present occasions that quickened moral passions and activities, rather than just conjectures about the reasons and motivations of action.

Even if these preconscious reference points were to be examined rationally, they probably would change only a little—not in any fundamental manner. They must be changed existentially, not merely cognitively, because they are held existentially. The participants are existentially confronted; their frames of reference are existentially reorganized; their decisions to act are fully existential.

The reference points (comparends) most visible in the interviews are embodiment, life-world, significant others, informing images (myths), and symbols of identity.

Embodiment as a Reference Point

The comparend function of embodiment surfaces when whites describe how they have overcome their prejudice toward blacks. Once this phenomenon is seen in white-black encounters, it is easy to discern in other situations.

From our earliest days, we tend to fear what we perceive as strange or alien. If we were walking down a street at night and suddenly, upon rounding a corner, bumped into an ET (extraterrestrial) creature, the psychological shock would be greater than if we bumped into a lamp post.

Since ET may be too familiar of an example, suppose that a tribe of beings has just broken through a wall in the unexplored depths of the Carlsbad Caverns. Their viscera are external to their skeletons; tiny eyes stick out all over; blue worms wiggle where we expect hair; they speak strange loud noises out of the wrong end of their bodies. We would be afraid; our skin would crawl. Until we had enough contact to establish that they are within a range of what we regard as human, we would treat them as potentially dangerous animals. Perhaps over a period of time we would discover that they are indeed more decent and intelligent than we are—that they are, in fact, a higher form of civilization. But it would take us a while to get over our dis-ease.

Science fiction routinely pictures this moral phenomenon. The TV show "Star Trek" shows "rocks" that have feelings of empathy, humanoids that turn out to be demons, and nonhumans that are loving. One beneficial contribution of science fiction is the repeated portrayal of humans interacting naturally with all sorts of fantastic creatures, such as the super-intelligent six-foot praying mantis, which laughs by clicking its mandibles, and repeatedly saves its human friend's life.

The differences among whites, blacks, and orientals is not so dramatic as that between humans and Carlsbad creatures or a praying mantis. Nonetheless these differences are sharply experienced in everyday life. Whites who have grown up isolated from blacks have a sort of gut-level anxiety in the presence of black bodies. Their body experienced-as-white becomes a comparend against which they unconsciously experience (and therefore judge) other bodies. They are not-like-me. If they are not-like-me, just how different are they? And, what further implications flow from the perceived difference?

Our own bodies set subliminal norms against which we measure other people to be older or younger, acceptable or unacceptable. We estimate our proximity to success or death by the age of people whose pictures appear on the business or obituary pages. We sit down on a subway seat next to a person who looks much like us—we are safe to ourselves, and think it probable that this like-me person is therefore safe too. This structuring of experience is subtle, elusive, and occurs at a gut level. Intellectually examining the way we structure experience helps, but this alone may not change its impact upon our consciousness. Many whites believed in equality in their heads long before they could get their emotions around that same reality. It took a long time before they could honestly answer

"Yes, why not?" to "Would you want your daughter to marry a . . . ?" The factor of "daughter marry a . . ." rather than "son marry a . . ." is an independently interesting, but associated phenomenon having to do with images of white female embodiment, black male embodiment, and body-rooted sexual anxiety so pervasive in our culture.

Because our bodies establish a frame of reference or a set of comparends through which we experience and judge the bodies of other people, we have trouble relating to someone whose face consists of ragged layers of scar tissue. A maker of prosthetic devices has described how his office waiting room would clear out in five minutes whenever a certain patient came in—a woman with a surgically removed nose, one eye with its eyelid and socket, and part of her forehead and right cheek. Her face triggered anxiety and gut-level repulsion; it was even more than other patients with similar problems could bear.

Children speak of people with black faces. The encounter is face-to-face, highly visible, and based on physical appearance. White children want to touch blacks' hair, and yet are afraid to. Many whites experience blacks—and the darker the skin the more it is true—as having a body different from their own. This sense of alienness provides a subtle, bodily experienced frame of reference within which it becomes easy to construct and perpetuate stereotypes. People will, of course, construct stereotypes with or without these differences. But the differences add a subliminal physical dimension to social perceptions. It was not terribly difficult for generations of whites to define blacks as subhuman. In Germany the perceived physical differences between Aryan and Jew heightened other factors, lending an extra push toward genocide. Touching the body is a small but significant limited-coverage insurance policy against genocide (which is one reason we need to keep school busing).

In the interviews, it is physical encounter that helps crack old prejudices. A white teen-ager was assigned a black roommate at a youth convention. When she woke up in the morning and rolled over to bump into a black body in bed beside her, her consciousness was jolted into awareness that this body was just like her own. In other cases physical proximity alone was enough to change perception: "She sat just in front of me, and I knew I could reach out and touch her hair." "I suppose the seventh grade was a key grade for me, because I can remember being in a class sitting behind a black person for the first time. Blacks and whites were together in physical education too. You dressed together; you exercised together." "I remember very well one night going to a party and dancing with blacks. I had never touched a black person, but I remember that very well." Touch, perhaps even more than sight, confirms that the other body is like-mine.

Though the white-black encounter is by far the dominant paradigm of alienation and acceptance that occurs at a physical level—gender, handicap, and age can also be noted. We tend not to notice gender-based body alienation because contact between the sexes is so continuous. Physical handicap, especially deformity (the elephant man) is a clearer case. The distance generated by any of these can be overcome by sufficient constructive contact.

Life-World as a Reference Point

Life-style and life-world also provide reference points that constitute or shape our frames of reference. Awareness and activation are often triggered by the discovery of the great difference between one's own life-style and someone else's. Life-world includes that circle of natural and human phenomena that surround one's everyday existence, providing it with a certain tonality and structure of meanings. It includes places of work and play, one's friends and acquaintances, one's activities and empathies. A person's life-world shapes her existential relationship to reality.

People often hold contradictory assumptions about the life-world of strangers—on the one hand assuming "they are like-me and therefore ought to be able to do what I can do or have done," and on the other hand assuming "they are so unlike me that they do not deserve the kind of treatment I deserve." On the first side, people sometimes unselfconsciously assume that the larger societal world is a series of diminishing mirror images of their own social world, as though it replicates the canons of their own social existence. Thus, middle-class people have trouble understanding poor people, because they overlay the taken-for-granted assumptions of middle-class daily existence on the imagined social world of the poor—"Let them eat cake." "If I can find a job, they should be able to find a job."

The significance of life-world as a comparend goes beyond such conscious interpretations. At some vague intellectual level, we are aware that somewhere "out there" people may be starving to death. But we are not fully, existentially, grasped by that reality because our daily life-world drowns those voices out. The comfort of middle-class existence blinds (perception), desensitizes (emotion), and "disinforms" (interpretation) our daily lived experience in such a way that that "out there somewhere" does not seem fully real. Our life-world is a powerful comparend, which gives normative shape to awareness and action.

The opposite assumption is that people who are "over there" are perhaps less than fully human. They are like-me, but not-really-like-me, or perhaps not-like-me-at-all—thus I do not apply the standards to their lives that I apply to my own life. One of Francisco Goya's etchings in the *Desastres de la Guerra (The Disasters of the War)* series portrays this assumption:

> There is, on the left, a tangled pile of bodies, a hooded figure lying face down, a child's corpse stretched out, and a figure with a hunger sharpened face wearing a peasant blanket with arms outstretched in entreaty toward the people on the right side. On that side two fashionably dressed women (long dresses, ribbons, and bows) manage to look away, while two men (cocked hats, spats, boots, riding crops) half look at the ragged locals. Beneath are the words, "Si son de otro linage"—"They are of another breed."[1]

Both the projection of one's own life-world on someone else, and the assessment that they are of another breed, rise out of a social-psychic distance between the self and the other. Even if the two parties inhabit much of the same physical space, as slaves did with their masters, a different meaning-space leaves the psychic distance intact.

The practical effects of the life-world as a comparend seem to function differently depending, in part, on the social space that exists between the comparend and the the comparee. We are more likely to compare ourselves with someone close at hand, than someone farther away. We measure our salaries against the people who work in our office more than against the Rockefellers or someone in abject poverty. We become more upset if someone close to our level and near at hand gets a $200 raise than if a truly wealthy person gets $2,000 more. (Of course we are also less likely to find out about the latter.) The situation of persons close at hand, or at least with whom we identify, affects us more.

Some important moral implications follow upon the observation that people judge others by themselves and themselves by others. Every individual who, for example, refuses to participate in the consumption-oriented ethos of American society can be a comparend to every other person with whom they come in contact. Those who work to change to a simpler life-style or who are engaged in political action often feel "What's the use! What good does my little bit do?" In addition to the cumulative effect of many individual efforts (many drops making a river), each individual is a potential reference point for others' decision making.

One participant recalled sitting at an alumni dinner next to a clergy friend who often supported social causes (as they are sometimes disparagingly called). The pastor did not eat her lettuce salad. It suddenly clicked in the mind of our participant, who was halfway through his salad, that the minister was silently supporting the United Farm Workers lettuce boycott. The minister, by example, had set a moral comparend over against which her friend measured himself.

No one else apparently noticed. Most people would have thought the gesture meaningless. Who benefits when the lettuce is thrown in the trash? In this case, the gesture of solidarity is more important than the lettuce. This fleeting experience helped the interview participant reorganize some of his own comparends. Every single one of us, in all of our deeds and lifeways, is a moral comparend for every other person—either positively or negatively.

The situation is even more pressing for persons who are identified as moral leaders—clergy and ethicists. The ethicist communicates not only ideas, but personal decisions, actions, passions, and life-style. The students unconsciously measure themselves against the lived-reality of the ethicist, not only the words. If the teacher talks about justice and inequality but does not act to alleviate them in some clearly perceivable ways, the students learn that justice and inequality are first and foremost linguistic events. They are things people talk about rather than things people do something about. If the students are seminary students, they take the linguistic event "justice" into their churches and preach about it, just as they have heard the teacher speak about it in the classroom, and then they wonder why people do not act on the message. Words beget words, in turn begetting more words. Perhaps the writer of the Gospel of John had something indeed when he described the advent of Jesus as the word becoming flesh, or as Goethe transformed it, "In the beginning was the act."

Students absorb not only the words but the contrapuntal message conveyed by the ethicist's actions and life-style. The issue here is not just integrity or hypocrisy; it is a question of what is being communicated—the incarnate comparend that the speaker becomes to the listener. A further and more important implication of comparends is that the society in which it would be easiest to become and remain moral is the one in which most people live a moral life-style.

The American life-world, shaped by advertising and the needs of the whole economic machine, is oriented toward a pattern of high consumption. Given the comparative nature of our consciousness it is easy to understand why upward mobility occurs. No matter where we are on the ladder, there are always people higher who act as comparends drawing us upward. The person who is rich can always begin to ascend a different ladder, for example, of power, where again someone will always be higher. Presidents of the United States (who may be both rich and powerful) compare themselves with other world leaders, and previous U.S. presidents. They want to be remembered as "better than."

The structuring of the American life-world is a massively convincing and seductive reality. But let us say that such a structure is patently immoral—that high consumption in a world where some people do not have the basic means of subsistence is evil. The change entailed in turning American society around would be enormous.

Imagine a society deciding that the best comparend would be good moral action rather than material goods, a society that could legislate morality by placing a limit on the available material comparends that encourage destructive patterns of consumption. Such a society would decide that for the good of the whole, no house could be built for over a certain (modest) set dollar figure; limits would also be placed on clothing, cars, and the many toys that clutter our lives. Likewise, the income gap between worker on the line, the supervisor, and the owner would be minimized.

Though this book has its origins and subject matter in the scattered moral experiences of solitary individuals, the results point not only to a pedagogy for small groups but toward the way a society needs to structure its moral reality. That structuring would require challenging the basic images and ethos—the assumptive frames of reference that underlie policy and practice.

> I am suggesting that the core of social change involves changes in the dominant meaning-structure of a collectivity's experience of the world; or, to state it differently, the problem of social change directly involves the question of under what conditions the constellation of perceptual images, meanings, presuppositions, and the like which make up a civilization's natural attitude comes to be displaced by another.[2]

Shifts in the ethos or fundamental meaning-structure of a society seem to occur in ways similar to those outlined in our treatment of the frame changes of individuals. Though it is risky to assume that the way individuals change also can explain processes of whole societies, there are discernible similarities. The black movement in the sixties confronted a large number of Americans for the first time on television with the effects of racism, causing at least some shift in the national resolution to do something. Public demonstrations in the Vietnam war era did not have quite the same effect. Though demonstrators kept the pot boiling, they did not really confront Americans with the disastrous effects of war. Pictures of the effects of napalm, the bombings, and reports of the My Lai massacre probably made more of a major contribution to an American consciousness. The shift that occurred then still accounts for the American view of small wars of containment. The collapse of the emperor system in Japan after World War II left a space partially filled by the Western technical project; currently two potentially disjunctive realities—traditional Japanese and modern technological values—contend for dominance.

While it is not my purpose to engage in societal analysis, the parallels seem to be there. There are those "fullness of time" moments of shock and awakening, which occur to a people, as well as to individuals. Each individual American can become a positive moral comparend adding one more witness, one bit of weight, which builds up breakthrough pressure upon the American ethos. Yet in the meantime, America needs to figure out political strategies, implementing these values at a public level, and speeding up the process of change.

Significant Others

Many significant others, especially parents, reference groups, and the victims, play into the awareness and activation experiences. Significant others are the internalized human voices that speak in our inner moral dialogue.

Much of the research on activism has sought to determine the kinds of socialization leading to radicalism, altruism, or activism. This research typically emphasizes the role that parents play in the making of an activist. One study correlated levels of commitment among civil rights activists with their parents' activism. The fully committed "had positive training for prosocial action;" the partially committed had "mixed or negative training," and those who only give money to good causes "had little or no training at all for prosocial action."[3] The fully committed "were taught not only to believe but to do."[4] Parents are among the internalized voices with whom one speaks. They are comparends of speaking and doing.

Many of our participants mentioned that their parents played a significant role in shaping their inclination toward activism. Christi: "I grew up knowing that everybody needs an equal shake, the Christian dogma. My parents were always taking people in. It's not a very hard transition to translate what I saw my parents doing." Shannon: "I've always had some social consciousness from the background of my family. My father was a minister, and my parents were active in the local NAACP chapter. There were things taught in our home that made us aware of problems that needed to be addressed. It seemed like all the hoboes used to come to our house, and my parents fed poor whites as well as blacks who were hungry. He sometimes took them into our home, gave them a meal, and helped them on their way." (People of an earlier generation were more likely to encounter hoboes wandering through the neighborhood seeking food and work. The demise of the neighborhood hobo has removed one sensitizing element from middle-class neighborhoods.)

Persons other than parents also could serve as significant role models. Mary referred to a socially active minister who had quickened their concern. Some described the actions of siblings. Ben mentioned that his younger brother was a leader in a Vietnam protest march in their hometown. "And it really made me start thinking that he was willing to step out. Here is this fifteen-year-old kid leading a march of several thousand people. It struck me hard that he could do that."

He's a really charismatic person. There was a riot in the high school, and the blacks and hippies were all ready to take the place down. Several people tried to calm the crowd in the school auditorium down. And my brother got on the stage and quieted them down, told them the riot squad was coming, which was nothing to mess with, and got all but a representative group to leave. Just super amazing. They got filed against and everything. Here's my brother doing this kind of thing because he believes there's hope for the world; things are going to change, and he's going to do them. I figured the least I could do is stand up for what I believed on one small issue.

Jean's brother had a collapsed lung and easily could have avoided the call to service in Vietnam. Instead he went to his draft board and refused to serve on moral grounds. He was sentenced five years in prison and was fined $10,000. While in jail he worked to organize and educate other prisoners. Jean became active in prison reform and party politics.

The category of significant others includes many public figures. Martin Luther King and Malcolm X's names were mentioned often. Cindy was impressed by a campus speech that she heard David Harris make.

I had been aware, but the incident which crystallized my feelings was when I heard David Harris get up and go through his experience in prison, the reasons why he had decided to be a conscientious objector, his whole being. He had a complete and utter sense of calm about him as he spoke. And yet he admitted that when he sent in his draft card just for spite he was a wild-eyed radical. And this calm and peace that he had, as he told in explicit detail what we were doing in Vietnam to those people and the kind of weapons we were using.

And to see the hurt in him and to know that he had laid his life on the line is when it crystallized. Up until that time I was still kind of playing the game—"Well, this is a neat thing to be in"—but at that point it was real. I had to stand with him. I had to stand against my government, against my father, against my family and say "This is what I believe in."

A feminist reference (identity) group is established when a woman discovers that she is not alone—that other women share her plight. Seeing her experience as like-theirs provides a community-of-identity that facilitates the emergence of her personhood; she judges her situation against that of someone similar.

Functioning as motivators and norms for actions, reference groups provide a repertoire of roles, vivid images, and symbols. They set a cluster of normative comparends against which a person holds herself accountable. One may identify with all sorts of groups, from the Daughters of the American Revolution to the New Left of the Second American Revolution—from the trash collectors union to the community of scholars. These groups or individuals give one's own identity a comparend against which to judge interpretation and action.

Significant others provide a basic orientation toward the world, including both concern for the other and a model of action in behalf of that other—both a way of viewing the social world and ways to gear into it. On the balance, the research participants recall their parents' deeds more vividly than their words. Doing is more compelling than speaking. Significant others might model personal effectiveness or personal responsibility; they might (in a given case) provide any of the elements of the activation experience discussed earlier. A major element in Ben's description of his fifteen-year-old brother's activities is a can-do—"If my brother at fifteen can do it, surely I can too." Jean's comments also emphasize her brother's courage and commitment.

Keniston writes that though significant others exemplify ideology and tactics, the chief characteristic they transmit is "charisma of commitment."[5] This element is certainly in evidence in the interviews—significant others not only provide patterns of performance to be mimicked but evocative images that inspire the imagination. Heroes and heroines, whether public figures or private acquaintances, fire up the imagination. They function symbolically. They infect people with "I want to do that too" and "I want to be like that." We aspire to do what they do, become the sort of persons they are, or, at least, think of our own lives as moving in the direction they symbolize. We compare ourselves with those moral exemplars who lure us on as human beings. A minimalist reading of the importance of such significant others emphasizes the can-do's they present. A maximalist interpretation pushes beyond doing to being— George: "My father was part of my image of who I can be."

There can, however, be a problem—to which person is one to listen? Hitler was a significant other to many people. The previous chapter spoke about responsibility-to, but not about to-whom. The problem deepens. An act of responsibility toward one person can simultaneously be an act of irresponsibility toward someone else. Stanley Milgram suggests that those who continued to shock the victim in his experiment may have seen themselves as being primarily responsible to the technician who was telling them to proceed and only secondarily responsible to the suffering victim. In the experimental conditions in which the technician left the room, obedience to his orders dropped sharply.[6] In experimental conditions in which the victim asked to be shocked and the technician told the subjects not to do so, they obeyed the technician. They were being obedient, and therefore responsible, to the authority figure rather than the victim.

In another research program done at about the time Lt. William Calley was being tried for participation in the My Lai massacre:

> Respondents were presented with the hypothetical situation of soldiers in Vietnam ordered by their superior officers to shoot all inhabitants of a village suspected of aiding the enemy, including old men, women, and children . . . when asked "What do you think *you* would do in his situation," 51% said that they would shoot and 33% that they would refuse to do so.[7]

The 51 percent probably did not feel their response was immoral or irresponsible at all. "In fact, this response represents what they would view as their moral obligation," precisely because of their interpretation of where responsibility lies in the situation.[8] In real life the intense pressures of the situation would probably lead more than 51 percent to shoot, and feel they had done the responsible thing.

It makes a great deal of difference—not only that one is responsible, but where the responsibility lies. It matters that some people are significant others, and it matters who they are. It is one thing to say that some people have castles as comparends while other people have slums—another to say which is better. It is fine that the participants think that they have grown morally, but then Hitler's SS no doubt thought that of themselves too. There must be something beyond self-perception and extant comparends that might guide us. An examination of sympathy or concern for the other opens up a path toward a human ethic.

Concern for the Other

In some ways the most significant others in the awareness and activation experiences are the victims. It is the plight of a victim, whether oneself or someone else, which often triggers an awakening experience. The potential activist responds to the situation of the victim. Responsibility is as much a response to persons who suffer as it is some quality of personality shaped by one's prior experiences. Instead of blaming the victim, the activist identifies with her. The suffering elicits more or less sympathy depending on where responsibility for the suffering is fixed. Karen discovered that "the fault was not in me." Blame, and therefore responsibility, lay elsewhere. There are other comments in the interviews about suffering where there was no reason. This is an attempt to fix responsibility. Deciding whether it is or is not her own fault that she suffers is one element in determining who is the victim.

The human capacity for concern for the victim, or identification with the other person has been called many things, among them sympathy, empathy, compassion, and love. In *An Inquiry into the Human Prospect,* Robert Heilbroner suggests that "the generalized capability of identification is the soil in which are rooted all possibilities of morality."[9] People, he said, tend to identify only with those close to them in space and time. Therefore there is little evidence that Americans will form that collective bond of identity with Third World nations and future generations that would lead us to change our lifeways enough to avoid the coming disasters. Future generations will be the beneficiaries or victims of such decisions.

The generalized capacity for identification has been a topic of philosophic debate under various guises since the beginning of philosophizing. Plato's *Lysis* is about friendship; friendship or "holding in common" receives more treatment in Aristotle's *Nichomachean Ethics* than any other topic. Adam Smith holds that sympathy is an important basis for making moral judgments about the other. We sympathize with someone we see on the rack by imagining what we would feel if we were in their place: "It is by changing places in fancy [imagination] with the sufferer, that we come either to conceive or to be affected by what he feels."[10] Sympathy is "fellow-feeling," which includes sharing the other's joy as well as sorrow. Sympathy in Smith's view is not emotional infection—a response to the other's emotion—it is our imaginative response to the situation we perceive someone to be in. Thus, we may feel joy for a person who is not at the moment joyful.

The most intriguing treatment of sympathy is Max Scheler's *The Nature of Sympathy.* Sympathy, Scheler writes, helps us enlarge our lives and "*transcend* the limitations of our own actual experience." It is second only to love. Scheler links sympathy with the alternation experience in citing the events of the Buddha's conversion: "A man who, having grown up amid luxury and splendour and all the amenities of life, was led by the sight of a few instances of poverty and sickness to discern and respond to all the pain and misery of the world, so that his whole life thereafter took an entirely different course."[11]

Scheler also noted "Tolstoi's story *Master and Servant,* which tells how the master's mean little heart is *opened,* after lifelong closure, in the act of his first experience of pure sympathy at the sight of his servant perishing of cold." Scheler uses metaphors like those in the interviews—"some trifle may open all our soul to human joys and sorrows for days and weeks on end, as if a light were suddenly shone, or a window opened, in a darkened room."[12]

Scheler understood himself to be building on Pascal's notion of the "logique du coeur"—the heart has its own way of grasping reality. "There is a type of experiencing whose 'objects' are completely inaccessible to reason; reason is as blind to them as ears and hearing are blind to colors."[13] Genuine sympathy is a direct emotional grasping of the meaning of the other person's experience as other; the experience is not reduced in some manner to one's own inner life. Scheler developed a typology of four kinds of sympathy— emotional infection, community of feeling, emotional identification, and vicarious participation in the emotion of the other, while remaining centered in one's own experience.

A. R. Luther describes Scheler's normative view of sympathy as "actualization descriptive of Being." Luther continues:

> Sympathy is a perspective or openness in and through which the other precisely as other is perceived in his absolute integrity of being, as a value in himself as man. The change of disposition or heart which constitutes sympathy as an openness towards the other as other is a creative act which penetrates into the density of Being, reaching a depth where the illusory monistic isolation of one's own being evaporates and one discovers himself beyond himself, that is, with another. . . . the change of disposition or heart towards another is spontaneous and involves a mode of knowing, namely, feeling, which is deeper than conceptual knowing and is only announced or mirrored in the latter mode of knowing.[14]

The interviews contain a variety of experiences similar to Adam Smith's description and Scheler's typology. There are experiences of the feeling-sorry-for sort. One person felt sorry for a man with a grotesque gait who approached him on the street. He felt sympathy, but also repulsion. Thomas reports feeling pain at witnessing the victimized people hauled into the emergency room of the hospital where he worked. "You feel the pain constantly there, because you're dealing with people who are victims of pain all the time." He hurt for and with them.

A variation of feeling-with occurred in those instances where people said they identified with someone who had been hurt. That identification was usually based on some commonality that existed between them. The person who identified with the students shot at Kent State was also a student. Several persons who had been discriminated against said things like: "I can identify with that, because that is where I had been."

There are also instances of "emotional infection." Many sixties and seventies activists were caught up by an emotional infection with the movements of the times rather than involved because of any lasting or deeply rooted symbolic commitment. It is no surprise that they moved on to other things when the movement slowed down and the times changed; they were enthusiasts. Therefore, their change does not invalidate the basic values or perceptions of the movement, as is commonly suggested.

"We consciousness" is also present in the interviews. People who have shared a common world, or common set of meanings develop a sense of we-ness. We-ness comes in a variety of forms: "You are not alone," "We're all in this together," "We can do this together." A genuine feeling of we-ness transcends one's I-ness, implicitly granting the other person credibility as being as much an I, as I am. In saying "we," a person grants the other some degree of equal status as a center of consciousness like one's own. Ben came to love the Appalachian children he worked with. The more he gained access to their life-world with its otherwise peculiar set of patterns and practices, the more he discovered a common humanity beneath the differences. The children became fully and existentially real to him. His and others' sympathy was of the became-sensitive-to or care-for sort.

Behind this variety of expressions lies a generic reality noted in each, but emerging most clearly in Al's interview. Al is white, over sixty, and has spent virtually all of his adult life working for the human good. His interview sums up many of these themes and suggests the generic pattern beneath them.

Most of my changes in social consciousness have not come through messages from the Holy Spirit in the middle of the night or being struck by lightning. They have been more gradual. They have come from contacts with other people, enlarged experience, and education.

Let me start with where I was. I grew up on a farm in Iowa. It never occurred to me that I would ever vote anything except Republican. Nobody in my family was anything except Republican. The only people I knew who were Democrats were an odd sort of people who were mainly Roman Catholics. To be a Democrat and a Catholic was to be the same thing, and I had no desire to join the group. So I cast my first ballot in a presidential election against FDR and for Alfred M. Landon. And we lost. In fact I think someone else voted for him, but I don't know where the guy lived.

In college what changed me to a New Deal Democrat was contacts with personal friends, who incidentally now are much more conservative than I am, but who became convinced that the Republicans were never going to do anything for anybody, and if the farmers weren't going to starve to death, they'd sure better get with the New Deal because this was the only place there was any concern for farmers. They influenced me to see that if I was going to look out for the self-interest of my kind of people, I would have to change to supporting the New Deal instead of supporting the Republican party. That this was where the action was.

Well, I can remember making the decision intellectually [frame disjuncture], but then I remember what a shock it was to me when I tried to get a summer job through Democratic patronage, through an uncle of mine who had always been a Democrat and a Catholic. He took me to this patronage boss to try to get this summer job and introduced me as a young Democrat. I hadn't yet identified myself publicly as a young Democrat. And I didn't get the job, but I can remember the shock of the experience of saying, "Well, I guess I am a young

Democrat [coming into focus]. **I guess I've moved that far."** So this was part of the process of change.

In seminary I studied with a well-known ethicist. Here was a man who was an intellectual, who had taken a much more radical position with regard to the economic establishment than anything I had taken up to that point. He had a lot of charisma, and had come out of a conservative background like I had. He encouraged us to do a study of migratory labor, and to read *The Grapes of Wrath.* This course was a very radicalizing experience for me; it opened up a whole new world that I had not been aware of. *The Autobiography of Lincoln Steffens* shook me up as much as any other one experience I had. It really sticks in my mind.

We took a class field trip to New York City where we visited the headquarters of the Communist party and interviewed William Foster who at that time was the head of it. Then, of course, we went through the tenements, the railroad apartments as they called them. I had just never dreamed that people lived like this. It was just kind of an eye-opener all the way around to see people living that way. Coming from a midwest farming area, I had no notion that people lived like that. So this was a very formative experience in terms of opening up my thinking. Now these things are shaped by later things.

A. J. Muste shared with us something I'll never forget—his experience of having gone through the Communist party and coming to the realization that it was not the answer. He was a very humble kind of a guy, and it was a very moving experience to wrestle through with him this experience he'd had being in and out of the Communist party.

I was a pacifist. We still were not in World War II; we were just six months or so shy of it at that time. When the war came, I had personal friends who refused to register for the draft and went to prison. I visited them out there in the federal prison. And this shook me up some to think that there were guys who took their absolute pacifism so far that they would serve a felony term rather than register for the draft.

Following the war I went to Africa. The whole experience in Africa was something of a radicalizing experience because you couldn't help asking yourself when you're in that situation how different your life would have been if you'd been born in central Africa instead of central Iowa. Those people didn't ask to be born there. I didn't ask to be born in central Iowa. What right did I have to be as different as I was from them? What responsibility did I have to change the situation there? I think your attitude toward your own country changes very much by living outside of it.

For a time I idealized America when I was outside it. You don't remember the warts; you remember the nice things. Everything in America gets to seem very good, and you contrast it with the inefficiency of things, the bad food and the uncomfortable living conditions in Africa. And you get to thinking how wonderful it would be to be back in America—if I could get into a drug store, a dime store, in a hardware store for ten minutes, it would save you weeks of work trying to find a few simple things that you need. So you get to thinking how wonderful it would be to have ice-cold drinking water, where you could go to the tap and drink it without having to boil it before you drink it, and you idealize the whole situation to where if you could just get back to America, everything would be perfect.

Then you come back to America, and you find that the stuff isn't all that good. The living conditions don't seem as wonderful as they did when you were suffering from the lack of them. And then you are thrown up against the very narrowness of your friends and acquaintances back here who don't even know that other world exists. They have kind of heard that it is there, but it doesn't bother them. They watch the soap operas and all they're interested in is the price of butter and eggs in Podunk, who is playing on the little league team and who is playing in the world series. Well, seeing fat, overfed, midwesterners that waddle and quack like ducks, and you think what in the world can people like this do to save the world? They are just a problem to it—totally involved in their own little affairs—and you get to hating them, just actually disliking the land of people you grew up with. I suppose because you identify yourself with where they are, because this is where you were. And then you hate yourself for having been there and you hate them for being there.

Then you begin to idealize the African situation now that you're out of it; how wonderful that was and how wonderful things are going over there, and how much wiser you were when you were in that setting than you are back here. You become a

**great world expert and that becomes idealized. I think in order
to maintain balance, a person would have to go back and forth
between the two experiences rather than out of one and living in
the other, and thus back from the one and living in the first one.
Because you always get a little out of touch with reality in the
situation where you are.**

**I know I had a friend that we knew who had done social
welfare work on the lower east side of New York. After she lived
a while in the barrios of South America, she went back to visit
those areas of New York and she said the slums were gone. After
living in a South American barrio they didn't look like slums
anymore, so the way things affect you is sort of relative to your
total experience.**

America and Africa alternately became comparends to each
other. I believe that Al's comment toward the end is
right—anyone who would speak meaningfully to the socio-
economic problem of this era must keep part of their
consciousness, perhaps even their body, in the communities of
the oppressed. The world looks and feels different from the
other side of the tracks, where there is more urgency about
change. The ethicist whose pervasive life-world is that of the
academy will have a difficult time keeping in touch with the
reality of other worlds. The minister whose psychic life is
surrounded by a middle-class congregation will lose touch with
the meaning of the communities of the oppressed. It becomes
difficult, if not impossible, to be moral under these
circumstances.

The seminary ethicist, A. J. Muste, and Al's pacifist friends
were all moral exemplars who inspired and modeled moral
commitment. The tenements and poverty in Africa presented
him with significant others who were victims. The new clue that
I find particularly interesting is Al's: "You couldn't help asking
yourself how different your life would have been if you'd been
born in central Africa instead of central Iowa. Those people
didn't ask to be born there. I didn't ask to be born in central
Iowa." Here we have a comparison based upon his awareness
of the accident of birth. His I-consciousness resides in a
particular sort of body in a given socio-cultural-historical
setting. But his I-consciousness just as easily could have been

born in someone else's body and culture—the many someones who are victims by accident.

This at first seems circular. If his I-consciousness had been born in their bodies, it would not any longer be his consciousness at all, but theirs—in fact, the very consciousness that they already have, shaped by their embodiment and culture. I do not see here a statement that he becomes the suffering other, or that he now sees the world fully from their point of view. He says that his body and consciousness are in principle, though not in reality, interchangeable with theirs; his life is in principle interchangeable with theirs. This principled interchangeability of consciousness at a formal level is then fleshed out or given some content as one goes on to imagine some part of what it is like to be the other person. The most crucial aspect of this, however, is the capacity to make connections between one's own experience and that of another person—that capacity to universalize from my consciousness and meaningful world to that of some other person(s).

"There but for the grace of God go I," people say. While this expression is rather thoughtless, suggesting that God is not graceful to the other person, it does catch that sense of the principled possibility of the interchangeability of consciousness. Another expression of this experience is found in the "Why me?" literature. The writings of those who escaped the German concentration camps alive are replete with "Why me—when all those thousands died, why did I survive?" There is no principled reason, just the accident of history.

Concern for the other is rooted at some level in the discovery of the other as other—not just an extension of oneself. The discovery that my mother had a mother, that perhaps my father had acne as a teenager begins to open up the possibility of seeing them not just as parents but as fully real human beings in their own right. The humanity of strangers is discovered in the opposite way. I experience them as other; what I need to discover is their likeness. Physical encounters teach me that, whatever other differences there are, their body is in some fundamental respect like mine—I discover that their suffering hurts them just as physical suffering hurts me. I do not need to undergo the same suffering. My bodily sensations are enough to clue me into the meaning of that suffering without having to experience it directly (though a very empathetic person may do that, too).

They not only have a body like mine, but they have a consciousness like mine, at least in the respect that it is a functioning awareness. Much of the content may be different, but they do inhabit a meaningful world—a world with significances of the same sort I experience. The constitutive thou-like-me-but-not-me experience grasps the other's existence as meaningful-to-them. They are like me, with respect to their humanity, though not their individuality. In fact, my consciousness is, at least in principle, interchangeable with theirs.

The experience of coming to self-awareness (I-am-me) finds its corollary in the discovery of the other as like-me. This discovery is not narcissistic or egoistic, for in saying "I could have been you," I am clearly separating myself from you and recognizing that I am not you. Thus, it is not self-regarding to say that I would not want you to be harmed just as I would not want to be harmed, for I remain existentially aware that your harm and my harm are two quite separate events. Neither is the recognition of the other intrinsically altruistic. It is simply a discovery of the nature of the human world as a social world. The possibility of that recognition is built into the structure of sociality itself.

Toward an Ethic of Sociality

This book can only suggest a direction for a normative construction based on these findings. That ethic would be an existential, a human, ethic, rather than purely rational ethic or even of the moral passions.

Many of our celebrations take shape around a recognition of the social character of human existence. The birth of a child (she looks like me) brings one more being into the societal fold, though it may take a long time before she is fully recognized as fully other—not just an extension of me. Pubertal rituals signify the coming to co-presence with the world of adults, like-us. A wedding is the symbolization of a consent to a particularly intimate form of co-presence—like-me, yet not me (not one flesh, but two whose worlds overlap in a particular way). A funeral threatens sociality, hints at its dissolution. As we face death, we recognize that we are in that moment like every other human being—rich, poor, famous—alone. Religious affirmations present reassurance of eternal sociality. These community events provide clues to our sense of interconnectedness, our aloneness together.

A human ethic would be an ethic of engagement—born, taught, and carried out in engagement with people and nature. It would be given to concreteness rather than abstractions, at least in its primary form. Its dialogue would be a conversation between persons and situations, a conversation not only of minds but of selves.

An ethic based on sociality would be an ethic of presence and conversation. Presence forces us to take the full texture of the other's reality seriously; conversation allows her to interpret that reality to us. It would be not only an ethic of knowing, but of conviction. Its first line of argumentation would be, if possible, presenting the victim rather than just talking about hypothetical victims. It would be an argument of human co-presence.

A newspaper article reports the suggestion of Roger Fisher, professor of law at Harvard, that is similar to the line of interpretation I am proposing.[15] Fisher notes the psychological distance of a president from the victims of a nuclear war. The president most likely would make a decision to push the button in a relatively "clean, air-conditioned room, surrounded by well-scrubbed aides, all talking in abstract terms about appropriate military responses in an international crisis."[16]

Fisher suggests that the codes needed to unleash the nuclear barrage be implanted "next to the heart of a volunteer, who would carry a big butcher knife as he accompanied the president everywhere."[17] If the president decided to push the button, he would first have to take the knife and with his own hands plunge it into the chest of the volunteer so that the capsule could be retrieved. The president would have to experience and take personal responsibility for the bloody death of at least one human being.

In "People of Vision" we suggest the form our argument would take to someone who had doubts about an ethic of presence and conversation:

Our first response would not take the form of academic and rational argument. Rather it would be to lead our questioner by the hand into the rooms of suffering, which we have seen, participated in, heard about, and can identify with. We would visit the slums of American cities and see the violence, the misery, the suffering—all part of daily life there under the aegis of our "good" system. We would sneak into a home in the barrio on Monday morning and talk with the children who are not in school because they do not have any shoes.

We would visit the farmers whose cattle were acting strangely after the Three Mile Island nuclear accident; talk with the Japanese mother whose daughter was born grotesquely deformed because of mercury pollution (and try not to avert our eyes from the daughter). We would make a short stop at the opulent home of the wealthy industrialist who claims his company isn't making enough profits, and then magically whisk to a Third World country where a family sells their daughter—hoping the sale will provide the financial edge they need, and thence to a Fourth World country where they wouldn't even bother because there isn't any hope.

We would dig coal in rickety gas-pocketed mines, inhaling traces of black lung disease. Then we would spend a day at Dachau, a day at Buchenwald, a day at Auschwitz—looking at the rooms filled with teeth, bones, and the dirty dolls once held by tiny human hands. We would stand before the photos of bone-jutting-through-skin humans—once just middle-class folks like us—and let ourselves cry . . . at least a little.

Finally we would point out to our questioner that the reason things look so good, so cheery, is that his life-style happens to be relatively free of such terrors. The whole world looks pleasant when the house is warm, the food is good, and the kids are well.[18]

As we stand with the victims and listen to their stories, our frames of reference might shift—the loudness of the normative voices within us would alter.

It is sometimes said that an ethic of presence, of concern, would leave one void of criteria. Would we simply be sympathetic toward a child molester or a murderer?—"I know how you must feel, and if I had been in your place I might have done what you did too." Coleen reported that her father had been killed on the streets of a southern city. The killer was caught. The family discussed what to do, and decided out of their compassion for the killer to seek a light sentence and rehabilitation.

Sympathetic listening to the murderer might lead to insight about appropriate rehabilitation; it might even shed dramatic light on major problems in the society and lead to social change. We might also present the murderer with the fully-textured reality of the person murdered and those who are left behind—he would view the body, pictures from the family album of the deceased on her fifth birthday, hear the first-person story and grief of the family. The killer would, if nothing else, be presented with reality in such a way that his humanity might be enlarged.

This ethic of presentation can be imagined at larger levels than face-to-face conversation. It takes a great deal of imagination for middle- or upper-class Americans to develop genuine concern for persons in slum barrios of Latin America. The media could remind us constantly of the human effects of the economic and social systems we have chosen. We could be confronted daily with the situation of suffering others (and provided clues about how to respond). "Commercial" messages might consist of the presentaion of those stories, myths, and symbols that quicken the moral imagination instead of the appetite to consume. We could be presented with opportunities to match our meaning qua-human with the experienced meaning (qua-human) of strangers, foreigners, and victims.

We could do even more than stand face-to-face, dialogue, and sympathize. We could fashion an ethical system with clear normative guidelines. But before the direction of such an inquiry is suggested, we need to remind ourselves that it is not necessary to say "Thou shalt not kill" to someone who has no desire or intention to do so, and precious little good to say it to someone who is determined to.

There would have to be a second order ethic to supplement an ethic of presence. Concern, grounded and constituted in the experience of awareness of sociality, becomes codified in moral stories, and maxims—society's extrapolation from (and reduction of) the insight that others are fully real and inhabit meaningful worlds. Not everyone has the insight, and those who do often lose sight of it. Insight must be institutionalized before we can deal with a host of anonymous relationships. Children have to be taught. People need moral guidelines to remind them and help them sort out what to do in specific circumstances.

This second order ethic would be built out of an exposition of the fundamental character of sociality. It would be an ethic of concern for oneself and others, an ethic of respect and responsibility toward human beings (including oneself)—qua-human (not qua-rational).

Societies as well as individuals need guidance in thinking through their laws and interrelationships. Furthermore, even at the basic level of one-to-one relationships, there remains an ineluctable alienation. Sympathy does not collapse one into the other; one never fully knows the world from the perspective of the other. The other person always remains separate, and thus has projects and perspectives that are bound to conflict at times with mine. What is true one-to-one becomes even more pronounced in larger groupings of people. A fundamental alienation is built into the very structure of sociality, calling for social means of regulating separateness in ways that enhance the common good.

If my consciousness is in principle interchangeable with someone else's, my status as "center of the universe" is relativized, though not lost. The other person is implicitly granted an equivalence of human be-ing. I can no longer justify a totally me-centric universe, but I do not lose myself any more than I would lose the other as a human self.

Fairness and equality are implicates of sociality. I tune into various other people and check them against my functioning comparends. (I notice that you have much more of life's goods than I have. What right do you have to possess so much when I have so little? What right do I have to possess so much when others have nothing?) The notions of equality and fairness are implied in the discovery of the other as like-me. If our consciousnesses are in principle interchangeable, then it is only the accidents of birth and socialization that make us different. We have, in principle, an equivalence of being, qua-human. Once that discovery is existentially affirmed, fairness and equality need no justification. It is inequality that needs to be justified (and there are elaborate systems for doing that).

Something is already granted in this second-order ethic when you agree to talk with me about it, perhaps to argue a point.

Once you have spoken to me as a meaningful-thou-like-your-self and expected a human response in return, you have already surrendered the most important point—namely, the right to treat me as anything less than fully human, less than a thou.

Once a person has said "Thou," and recognized that person as a human-like-me, he has already implicitly granted status qua-human—that they should be treated by standards of equality and fairness. An ethic grounded in sociality would spin out the implications of concern for the well-being of oneself and its corollary, concern for the other. This concern can be described as a perceptual, intellectual, and emotional leaning toward the meaningful reality of self and other, or it can be described as love.

Such an ethic would, for example, present norms that say murder is bad because the murderer is not treating the other person like a fully constituted human being, and as a result, has dehumanized himself to some degree. In not caring for the neighbor, one is implicitly surrendering care for oneself. Such an ethic would consist of an elaboration of "Love your neighbor as yourself." The next question indeed is, "And who is my neighbor?" The answer is everyone, but especially the victim.

The victim receives special attention because she has been deprived—whether by nature (blind, crippled, etc.) or by society (racism, sexism, colonialism)—of some significant part of her ability to respond as fully social. She has been deprived of some of the basic rudiments required to interact in a fully-present manner suggested by the structure of sociality. Such an ethic would direct attention first toward the victim—it would seek to redress wrongs and actualize the implicit structure of human existence as social. Responsibility is, first of all, response to the victim. "A [person] was going down from Jerusalem to Jericho, and he fell among . . ." (Luke 10:30). A person who becomes committed to social justice moves from charity to solidarity with the oppressed.

MEMORY
COME ALIVE

The question "*Why* did you become involved?" may elicit a different response from "*How* did you become involved?" The first invites an answer in which involvement is justified—a cognitive statement about justice or equality, or the projection of a hope for the future—"I have a dream. . . ." The *how* question encourages a look into the past, a description of experiences leading to involvement. The present interviews contain justifications and visionary statements, but focus on descriptions of prior experiences. They move on the boundary between personal history and poetry, between self-story and self-drama.

The life history or autobiographical interview has been part of the research sociologist's repertoire at least since the Chicago school studies of the twenties and thirties. It has been lauded by qualitative social scientists as providing a comprehensive and fully textured picture of a social reality, and castigated by quantitative social scientists for not telling how extensive the phenomenon is. The latter say its subjectivity renders conclusions narrow and tentative at best. However, as I have studied the interviews, listened to other conversations along the way, and compared them with what journalists, social scientists, and philosophers write, I have become more convinced of the value of the interview-autobiographical approach. There was a cumulative sense of the validity and authenticity of the interviews and interpretations I have based on them. Several of those who were interviewed read a near-final draft of the manuscript and reported that the interpretations seemed fitting.

Autobiographical interviews are composed of interpenetrating acts of presentation and recall. The speaker reconstructs a story of the self. But the construction, based on memory, is simultaneously an act of presentation to the interviewer. The presentative act takes the interviewer into account, to some extent. The interviewer sets the frame of reference, but the respondent decides how to paint the picture within that frame. The respondent describes, relives, explains, interprets, and justifies courses of action.

Certain structural elements can be noted in the interviews. The response is a story, perhaps even a drama, with a beginning, middle, and end. The beginning is the selection of a dominant theme or plot, the setting of a context for action. The story is told from the perspective of the central character, the respondent's life and body with its comings and goings as the center point.

Other characters are introduced not so much as individuals, but as roles within the story. Sub-themes are woven in as the plot is developed. The person makes an effort to present events in chronological order—when something is accidentally omitted, the speaker tries to go back and insert it into the place where it belongs. The austere economies of time collapse the flow of experience into bounded events. The presentation is aimed to inform, and probably entertain, the interviewer as an audience. The interviewer is invited by the respondent to get into the story. The thematic unity is built through a series of episodes to a climax and a denouement.

The genre "story" has recently received much attention in theological circles. It is tempting to see the respondent's tale as a story of the self. The story is so sparse, so lean and ascetic, however, that I am inclined to see these interview-performances as closer to drama than story, to poetry than prose. The luxury of slow development and detailed description is not present. Instead we have a spontaneously fabricated, tightly drawn, carefully scripted part of the drama of a person's own life—itself the dramatic center of human experiencing. The interview is part-presentation, part-performance. The performance carries the connotation of drama.

The drama is not as evident in the printed text as it was in the original telling. If tape recordings, or video tapes were inserted in a pocket at the back of this book, the reader could hear people tell personal stories filled with meaning and emotion. The research participants described important life-shaping experiences. They gesticulated excitedly as their voices rose and fell with dramatic passion.

These are moral dramas; for whether or not they invoke the language of justice, they are set within a general context of doing good, helping other people, or changing the world for good. They express legends and myths of the self's identity, and point toward symbolic centers of the self's existence.

The interviews both do and do not tell us why people become socially involved. In a study of the genesis of social involvement, one is first inclined to look for those antecedent causes that lead to consequent actions. Most studies have proceeded exactly this way, studying values, early socialization, or immediate situational factors, which elicit certain kinds of behavior. There is no predictable path of causal relationships one can follow to guarantee that a person will want to act in certain ways, short of brainwashing or posthypnotic suggestion. That contained in the interviews is more significant than antecedent-consequent analysis provides. There we find a residue of meanings which, on an ongoing basis, continues to bubble up through consciousness to enliven a life-style of commitment to social change. These remembered meanings are based on experiences powerful enough that they stuck hard in their consciousness. The capacity to recall such experiences suggests that the original experiences continue to inform their self-understanding.

The experiences related in the interviews are reported memories—echoes of experiences that happened in other times and places. We do not hear or see them in the living sound, color, and splendor of their original occurrence. Instead we have the staggered reverberations of original experiences bounced across successive hills of experience.

Mnemosyne, the Greek goddess of memory, held an important place among the gods and goddesses. Her mother was Uranos (heaven) and her father earth (Ge). Mnemosyne and Zeus were the parents of the nine muses—the source of creativity in science, art, history, and literature (especially poetry). The Mnemosyne myth suggests that memory is foundational to the varieties of human experience and expression.

Without memory there is no music, for it is the retention of tones—from one note to the next—that makes melody possible. Without memory there are no images for poetry to invoke. Without memory there is no history, personal or collective, and thus no identity. All recall is proto-history; memory is to the self what history is to society.

Franz Kafka was once asked whether he recalled the old Jewish quarter in Prague. His answer summarizes our own experience—although something may have disappeared physically, it lives on in our images and meanings. " 'In us all it still lives—the dark corners, the secret alleys, shuttered windows. . . . Our heart knows nothing of the slum clearance which has been achieved. The murky old Jewish town within us is far more real than the new hygienic town around us.' "[1]

Reality is not just a function of out-there objects. The realities guiding our lives are those inner meanings that spill out into activity. To recall a memory is to link some part of present experience with some fragment from prior experience. To speak a memory is to share that fragment with someone else. Remembering is an interpretive act in which the present moment becomes quickened with the vitality of a meaning originally constituted in a past moment. Remembering as a matching of past and present creates the possibility of symbol-creation, an expression of the muse.

Levels of Recall

A close examination of the interviews suggests there are varying levels of recall. Obviously, people have differing capacities for remembering things. The only significant event that one sixty-four-year-old male could remember from his early years was: "My parents were moderately conservative. My dad was a Republican. I was just thinking this morning that on the farm where my dad was brought up, they called the privy the Democratic headquarters." On the other hand, a seventy-four-year-old woman was able to recall large chunks from the years she had worked in the labor movement, her lobbying for child welfare legislation, and experiences in which exposure to extreme poverty had deeply impressed her.

Along with one's capacity or incapacity for remembering, the interviews show varying levels or depths of recall. The metaphors "level" and "depth" suggest that one has to dig deeper and deeper in memory to describe what is retained there.

The first degree or level of recall is the identification of some experience as meaningful. People recall some event or brief period in their life as being important, but do not remember exactly what happened. Dorothy recalls that reading *The Autobiography of Malcolm X* was significant in shaping her racial awareness, but could not remember any of the contents. Belva recalls that a major change in her awareness took place at a summer church camp, but can not isolate any specific event that occurred there.

At a second depth of recall, people sketch the bare bones of an event without being able to recover it fully. One participant remembers having been struck by the cover title of early 1960s *Ebony* magazine—"The White Problem in America." He recalls having thought, "Yeah. That is right. That's the way it is. I never thought of it that way." But he couldn't recall whether he was alone or with someone, what sort of building he was in, or even the city in which the experience occurred.

At deeper levels of recall, people's descriptions are more fully fleshed out—they remember times, places, and can describe events in great detail. Claudia vividly describes a walk she had taken down a street of poverty.

The roads aren't paved. There's no curbs and gutters. Even if it was paved, it's completely broken apart. It's absolute chaos.

You're walking down the street. It is Johnson Avenue. They're dirty, some sidewalks, some not. Broken busted glass strewn on them. Many of them dirt gouged out. It happened to be after a rain. Great swills of mud. The broken limbs of trees. Stuff piled around.

I am mainly trying to keep from being too muddy at first. But you begin to wonder to yourself. How many people live on this street? How long has it been like this? Now I understand what chuckholes and potholes mean. How come there are so many big police dogs savagely barking in the back of every yard behind fences? Or, if you go to knock on the door, these big dogs throwing themselves against the door snarling. What is the crime rate here? Why is every door locked in the middle of the day, and every screen has a latch, right? Why do people talk to you through the door first without opening them? What's going on in there that this is a way of life, that they're barricaded in? How come there are so many unemployed males at any time of the day when you go down there?

I walked a precinct on the southwest side of town. Again, unpaved roads, hot and dry, old people. Some of the homes fairly neat, but run down. You go in them. I can remember one quite distinctly. A woman, probably in her eighties, who was blind, living with another woman, bedridden, I presume in her eighties also. Almost all the furniture gone from the house. I'm assuming that it's been sold off a piece at a time to pay for medicine or food. I mean, just a plain floor with one table and a straight-back chair, and one second-hand cupboard and bureau and a bed stuck right in the living room. The women were in ill-fitting, second-hand cotton print dresses, which kind of draped on them. There's no money left in that family. They're trying to live with some dignity.

At deeper levels of recall, verb tenses frequently change from past to present, "there" places take on a "hereness," and pronouns shift from "I" to "you." John Howard Griffin shifts to "and suddenly" you "were sitting in those rooms and" you "became aware. . . ." These pronoun shifts are different from the impersonal use of "you" as an equivalent for "and suddenly" one "was. . . ." It is as though the storyteller is perhaps trying to draw "you," the listener, inside the rooms, or down the street with him. Because the teller gets into the subjective vivid present of the original experience, there is more of an investment in pulling the listener inside. Perhaps this is an unconscious strategy to get the hearer inside the meaning that experience has for the speaker—by having them live through it together.

At the deepest level of recall in these interviews, people move from reproducing to reliving the experience. They slide gradually deeper into the existential impact of the experience. They dwell in memory as though it were a fully textured present reality—an experience from the past "lives again." At one point I asked Belva if she wanted to role-play an event she had just described vividly. She said no; it had been an unpleasant experience when it occurred years before. Merely describing it had brought back as much pain as she cared to deal with. Role-playing would make the experience more lively than she was ready to face.

Recall Shapes the Recalled

1. Recall shapes memories or retrieves experiences in thematic unities. In an interview, the initial theme is set by the questions the interviewer asks. In reverie, events spring serendipitously out of the past. But in the interview context, they are lifted out. The questions initiate themes around which certain events, rather than others, are drawn out of the past. The interviewer's questions provide a string on which the respondent threads the beads of experience, making a necklace of the self. The initiation of a theme as a probe into memory creates a synthesis of identification. Serving as a kind of mental stimulus, the theme or question shoots like an impulse through consciousness, striking sparks at intervals and in places where something of similar import is stored.

The experience of time or temporality also molds experience. People present autobiographical events in the order in which they were originally experienced. These presentations aren't strictly chronological, but experienced and remembered chronology, sifted out in terms of the question at hand.

The process of recollection and presentation also tends to present events in their spatial referents, social connections, and from the perspective of the embodiment of the recaller. Events are located in specific spaces. Persons describe going places in terms of the original positionality and motions of their bodies, such as, "we went over there," "up there," "back home."

Events are not merely reported as "I" events, but in their social dimensions.

"Naming" is a curious aspect of some of these ordering principles. People seek to locate events in space, time, and their social dimensions by naming streets, dates, and persons. Considerable energy often goes into searching memory to recover exact names and dates. The curiosity lies in the fact that names would mean nothing to the interviewer. It really does not matter whether the old school administration building was located on Commerce Street or Red Oak Drive. Nor does it matter whether the person met there was Larry Rackham or Jean Moberly.

The desire to name things might be the respondent's attempt to establish credibility in the eyes of the interviewer. By citing names, the person establishes that he or she has a good capacity for recall, and thus can satisfy one of the interviewer's implicit concerns. However, I suspect that this desire to tack down such specific things as names is done more for the satisfaction of the speaker than to please the interviewer. There is a need to tie down, to bind, to fix some parts of the story in consciousness. The speaker needs to prove that important names are recallable. The speaker is not just making a case for the interviewer, but is involved in an act of reexperiencing and authenticating the memory. The addition or subtraction of minor details shapes the interpretation being given, which implicitly gives it greater credence and justification.

Our memory of ourself grounds our perception of ourself. We are, in a sense, the person whom we remember and envision ourself to be. I am a memory come alive. The naming of names, dates, and addresses becomes important because to lose these facts is to lose part of our own person—when we forget those details we fear losing part of ourselves. To name is to be able to claim, assign meaning to the remembered, and retain one's own identity.

2. Recall retrieves and endows meanings. It is interesting to note that the levels of recall are ordered in terms of meanings. One first recovers a meaning, then the meaningful event, then the fuller experience of the event. At the top or most recallable level is a meaningful event without much context, personal involvement, or degree of detail. Each level of depth not only

uncovers more detail, but leads the respondent to dwell deeper and deeper in consciousness. The deeper the dwelling, the fuller the recovery of meaning. Once the theme has been cued by the interviewer, recall is structured in terms of human meanings—the throwing together or symbolic matching of present and past meaning structures.

Recall constitutes the meaning of an experience. Events and an interpretation of their meaning are separated in time, if only by moments. When we are in the immediate flow of an experience, it commands our attention fully. When we reflect on the experience, we assign it some meaning in the overall scope of things. Previously constituted meanings may be recovered or even constructed for the first time—if this is the first time the speaker has stopped to reflect on the experiences in question.

Some things are remembered because of the intensity generated when they first happened. It is not hard to recall one's first surgery, though repeated surgeries may blur together. Other events are remembered because they connect with some vivid part of our present set of life experiences. The experiences recounted in these interviews express this duality. They are explosions in consciousness, constituting a commitment to social involvement, and they are retrieved in memory because (in reverse temporal order) the present life-style continues to be sustained and informed by those experiences. In matching past and present, they are really proto-symbolic moments.

The process of recalling something, then, is a powerful intersection of those sedimented meanings that are the residue of a past now formally gone, and those meanings which daily continue to reconstitute ongoing life-choices and commitments. As experience flows downstream through our lives, some moments pass around the bend and are forever lost. Other moments have greater weight. They settle to the bottom and continue to influence the flow passing over them. This settling down constitutes the level of our most important meanings—our impressions of life and death, of temporality and sociality, of meaning and meaninglessness. These shape our lives, creating eddies and flows, rapids, bends, and straight places.

The process of interpretation is ongoing. New experiences may lead one to interpret old experiences in new ways. What once looked like a moment of immense personal tragedy, later may appear as a turning point toward greater growth. In the interviews, blacks typically recall some moment they were able to reinterpret individual experiences of personal suffering, as not just isolated private tragedies, but as the results of systematic cultural discrimination. Women with the "disease that knows no name" came to see that it wasn't just they who were to blame for the malaise that pervaded their lives, but rather a system of cultural oppression. Both of these reevaluations are based on the ongoing process of reinterpretation of the self.

Recall of the sort that took place in these interviews is something more than dusting the artifacts stored in the corners of one's mind. It is an act of reinterpretation, of reperceiving Grandma's ugly old wooden chair as a quaint antique. Recall is a highly interpretive process. It selects one series of moments from the many available. This act of inclusion and exclusion, even though done spontaneously, is an act of judgment. Recall is also interpretive in its capacity to shape events in ways that give them one, rather than another sort of meaning. Recall is a meaning-endowing as well as a meaning-retrieval operation.

3. Recall presents imploded experience. Recollection not only creates unities of meaning out of past events, it separates the past into discrete moments called events. Life experienced originally as flow is memorially experienced as discontinuous. The acts of remembering and forgetting disrupt flowing sequences, putting boundaries around them and turning them into events. Thus, when participants recall experiences from their past, they retrieve a series of events—what Nabokov calls patches of the past. The interview is a self-conscious stitching together of such patches, creating interpretive quilts made up of bits and pieces of memory's cloth. Said Christi, "I don't think it was as conscious and precise a thing as I make it out now."

Complex experiences are reduced in the mind to typifications—mental constructs that help us distinguish this type of thing from that type of thing—a tree from a bush. We typify not only other events and people but ourselves. Several varieties of typifications can be found in the interviews—characterizations, caricatures, myths, and symbols. The latter are more than mental constructs, although they seem to arise in typifications.

References to oneself are such things as "I am the sort of person who. . . ." "My whole purpose in life was to be a mother." Part of our self-understanding is comprised of typifications of the sort of person we are—dumb, tall, friendly. These typifications are built up out of our ongoing interactions with other people. One set of such typifications involves images about our political stance. Several people summed up who they were (with regard to the questions at hand) in terms of their voting record. Voting is a moment when each of us sums up our values and perceptions in one decisive act of pulling a lever. There is little room for subtleties and ambiguities. Since voting brings one's political identity into sharp focus, some people mark their political evolution by changes in voting patterns over the years, especially presidential elections.

Another form of self-typification goes beyond characterization to caricature:

Thomas: When I started college, I was an ultraconservative fundamentalist. I didn't drink, dance, swear, smoke, go to shows, play cards. I hadn't been to a movie or had a drink until I graduated from college.

Christi: I had a college education, children, and a husband who was good to me and earned lots of money. We had two cars and a big house on the hill. And that didn't hack it. That wasn't nearly enough to make me happy. For the longest time I assumed being unhappy was my failure. If I have everything it takes to be happy and I'm still not happy, then the fault lies within me.

Respondents collapse their experience (including their past identity) into cultural typifications as "supermom" or a "gung ho son of a bitch Vietnam airborne parachutist infantry officer." These caricatures are spontaneous presentations of the myths anchored in consciousness about their own private pilgrimages through life.

Ongoing life experience collapses the full texture of lived-events into black holes of experience that contain invisible sources of power and implode many things into one intense thing. Recall retrieves these imploded meanings. "Memory . . . imports the past into the present, contracts into a single intuition many moments of duration."[2] It was not at all unusual in the interviews to discover a "summing up" experience—one particularly significant experience that symbolically caught the meaning of many like experiences. That experience was "something I can look at symbolically," said Jorge, reflecting on the relative place of a reported experience among unreported ones.[3]

This collapse of experience is more than cognitive; it carries heavy emotional components. As the imploded experiences are retrieved by memory, some of their power radiates through the language, gesture, and intonation of the speaker. The interview elicits a species of subjective reflections, described as "concerned with self-conscious surreality and one's *personal* investments and involvements."[4]

This concentration of experience creates an intensification of the recalled moments—a concentration of power and a summing up of meaning within their center. Among those interviewed, some of the more dramatic respondents moved from caricature to myth and symbol. These myths of the self are not merely mental images but "synthesize our views as emotional judgments into a coherent dramatic framework, organizing the dull facts of the world into the excitement of personal involvement and meaningfulness."[5]

4. Myth, symbol, and identity. Myths of the self are grounded in some episode in one's personal history. As the episode continues to inform one's perception, interpretation, and action over time, its meaning can become intensified—as relived in imagination, the story/drama infuses transcendent meaning into daily life. "The figures of myth touch the lives of individuals with transforming power."[6]

The myth is chosen from the pool of myths and symbols available in cultural and religious sources. One woman attorney imaged herself as a budding female equivalent to civil rights lawyer William Kunstler. Others mentioned Don Quixote, Albert Schweitzer, and Martin Luther King, Jr.—not so much as historical personages, but as the myths and symbols they had become. These myths yoke self-identity with other human symbols of concern and involvement. The speaker is dialogically relating to others who identify with the same myths, through cultural imagery. We can learn something about people by discovering the myths they identify with, and conversely we can learn something about the meaning of cultural myths by the uses people make of them.

These myths unfold symbolic meanings. "A symbolic event crystallizes and bears a moment of vision through the viscissitudes of temporal occasions. In this sense it constitutes and bears a history."[7] A symbolic order sums up a past and anticipates a future. It is a ground or framework of meaning for an individual. "The symbolic order comprehends and penetrates the subject's life-world, and endows that world with meaning for him."[8] People are meaning-creating, meaning-seeking beings. Meanings are imaginatively rehearsed in myth and symbol. Thus, imaginative recovery of the self is on the boundary between history and poetry.

When Gene was asked verbally to sketch a picture of his changes of consciousness, he first describes the evolution of his changes and then refines the description into the language of myth and symbol. His comments include images of awareness and activation.

As a child I was given the values, which left me open to that kind of consciousness. I was also given the ability and opportunity to be able to think and evaluate, and take a hard stand in a very supportive and creative atmosphere, which I think was probably the major factor in where I am right now.

Then in the sixties I was saturated in church youth groups, in church conventions, through television, through school, through the whole social awareness thing that went on during the sixties about civil rights. And I got a lot of emotional and factual input during that stage.

I think the next stage was my emotional response to all of that. Somehow going to college and all of a sudden realizing that all of the values I held and all of the stuff that was going on in the world didn't meet up. They didn't go together. And so I responded emotionally.

At the same time because of my intellectual needs, I supported my emotions with a bunch of facts. But I was committed to be emotional, committed to any action in which I could express that emotion. It was almost a martyr complex. "I'm so good," you know. I got a lot of strokes out of being a martyr. And although I think I've become more and more realistic about that, it lasted for two or three years.

And then there was a period when McGovern lost that I gave up. There was a period of complete and total "Tell the world to ———— off cause it's not going to change anyway, and I don't care anymore." And yet I did care, and I hurt. And then through Watergate I was very vindictive. You know, "I told you so!" [laughs]; "We've got him by the balls now." And it was like "By God I was right so you get the ———— off of me."

And yet through that I went back into the emotional thing, to getting involved in every issue, no matter what it was, gung ho and play the martyr bit again. And then just lately learning the tools and the reality of what it's going to take to do something about all that emotion. And now I have the beginnings of some very hard-core realistic understanding of what it's going to take to change things.

Q: If you had to draw a picture of yourself in each of these stages what would the picture look like?

The first stage is a child when the values were being fed to me. I was like a receiver, very open, but a mechanical device, which interpolates the sound. I received it and clarified it and was able to think about it, because of the supportive atmosphere I was in. The second stage, in the early sixties, I was a sponge. I didn't really evaluate any of that knowledge, I just soaked it all up.

The third stage when I finally started putting all that together and I became a warrior. The symbol I would use is a don—a Spanish loyal soldier—which is the mascot of the high school which I went to. We had a mascot of a guy who is standing there with a sword in his hand running out with his sword to defend and to beat off foes. And I wore my high school ring which had that symbol all through college. Everything I did was right down that line. You know, take the sword and whip off the enemy [laughs]. You know that's a bad example to use when you're fighting against the Vietnam war [laughing]. And it's very true because a don represents more than a soldier. It represents truth and wisdom, caring, a very supportive high school atmosphere in which the principal emphasized over and over and over the thirteenth chapter of Corinthians, and his whole life was just love, love, love.

The next stage I think I would draw a picture of my back and walking away. I know the symbol! There was another show that really had an influence on me. It was called *And Then Came Bronson*. It was about the newspaper reporter whose best friend committed suicide by jumping off the Golden Gate bridge. They'd built a motorcycle together. And Bronson got on that cycle and just took off; it was like, "I have to get away. I have to go out and find who I am." And I remember down in my guts, during that time after McGovern lost, feeling over and over again that I wanted to tell the world to go get ———— and get on that motorcycle and just take off by myself and just be. Bronson was a very quiet, very aware kind of person. And I think that awareness was a searching. I would see myself in the picture as sitting on that cycle riding off into the sunset as a form of searching and as a form of escape at the same time.

The last one, the vindictive stage—I was probably back with the soldier, only this time probably not going out to fight the cause, but coming in to poke at the enemy and say, "Ha, ha, I've got you now."

The sixth stage is one of, I'd almost say, a wholeness. I'd draw a circle because I still have that emotion which drives me to the social concern, but I have a realistic evaluation of what that is and how you change it. And I have regained my concern and love for the persons who are involved in that.

Gene's images evolve from sponge through don to a circle of wholeness (a common religious symbol). Dramatic self-imagery has the power to shape and sustain identity. Self-images are at the core of our consciousness of ourselves and others. Our moral identity is formed in symbolic moments. Recall "is an intrinsic binding together of past and present in the identity of the self that both experienced the past event and now recollects it."[9]

Symbolic moments from the past intermingle with cultural myths to form the myths of self identity. "Our mythologies define our conceptions of ourselves, as heroes or as martyrs, as 'goodhearted but misunderstood' or as talented but unappreciated, as lovable but unloved, as gallant or as cowardly, as generous or as miserly."[10] In the interviews, they are myths of social concern and political involvement. Spawned in change-of-frame, change-of-symbol experiences, they have become consciousness-shaping, meaning-bearing, identity-sustaining, world-changing events.

EPILOGUE: REFLECTIONS ON PEDAGOGY

No single pedagogy will produce guaranteed-or-your-money-back activists. Human beings are a variable lot; they respond to different things. Some are grasped by noble causes; others just want a good excuse to get out of the house. The participant who claimed to have hijacked a plane to Cuba illustrates some of the complexity of human decision making.

The thing that really made me aware of things and really shocked me happened in my hometown. Here came a white family—and I've seen them several times since that time, but I remember first seeing them—and they had no shoes and were super skinny—malnutrition. They looked like they were in their sixties, but I imagine they were really in their forties; just poverty-stricken-looking people. The boy and the man had ropes for belts; the whole family had teeth that were curved like fangs. And I said to myself, "That's ghastly. How could that be?" And I said to myself later when I thought about it, "These are human beings just like anybody else. How can they be like that? Why is it like that; why should it be like that; and what can be done about it?" And I said, "Now here's the United States that is the wealthiest nation in the world, and yet here are citizens that look like that and there's nothing can be done about it. It's outrageous!" When I looked at politics and the politicians, the

money being spent on the Vietnam war, the hypocrisy, the shiny cars and say "What are they contributing? Nothing. Absolutely nothing."

He saw the movie *Dr. Zhivago* and began to read about Russian peasants and the Communist revolutions. He was appalled at the atrocities being committed in the Vietnam war. He got the idea that hijacking would be a "revolutionary blow," and it would enable him to "go to Vietnam and act as an interpreter or in some function similar to that for the Vietnam people." In fact, he could not speak Vietnamese and had very little idea what he would do when and if he got there. One night his father and stepmother, who were getting a divorce, had a fight about his having moved back into the house. "And so I decided, 'Well I helped break up their marriage which wasn't that great but at least it was theirs, and I can't get along with them, and I believe like I believe,' and the next day I did it!"—the hijacking.

He hijacked a plane to Cuba because he couldn't afford to buy a ticket, and because it was not easy for U.S. civilians to get into Vietnam. He imagined that if somehow he got to Cuba, they would help him get to Vietnam. As it turned out, the Cubans put him in jail.

Ostensibly most of the things that this book suggested might lead to social involvement happened to him. His awareness grew out of confrontation with poverty and the atrocities of Vietnam. It was through a series of comparisons—"the wealthiest nation in the world," and "the shiny cars"—that the contrasts were heightened and took on moral significance. He said to himself, "These are human beings just like anybody else," a variation of the principled interchangeability of consciousness, or the awareness of human qua-human, described earlier.

There is no way to be certain what would have happened had his parents not had the fight that became his tipping point. Human motivation is complex and variable—people respond for reasons that elude discovery. Nonetheless, it is reasonable to believe that a pedagogy for activation is possible.

A pedagogy for social action would help people become aware and involved. Awareness can arise out of the experience of seeing people needlessly suffer or by bonding with them. Face-to-face confrontation with the suffering person can lead to existential immediacy, which creates breakthroughs. Listening to that person's story undercuts negative stereotypes and enables one to be more sympathetic. People can also be drawn inside the meaningful world of another person (whether victim or not) through autobiographies, biographies, and novels. The voice of the other person has to become as loud as possible to drown out the blaring noises of a self-centered consciousness.

Confrontation needs to be accompanied by interpretation. The sufferer's victimization needs to be pointed out. Comparisons need to be made between the situation of the would-be activist, and those who suffer. Then persons should have the fundamental accident of their birth interpreted to them: There but for the accident of birth go you. A view of the interconnectedness of human beings, our fundamental likeness qua-human, our intrinsic sociality, would be presented: "There, in effect, go I."

The would-be activist would be helped to acquire a sense of personal effectiveness by participating in successful social change events. He would learn *how to,* that he *can do,* until he felt *at home* in the world of social action. She would learn that victims can be helped, and that she can be the one who helps. Would-be activists would learn that they have a personal stake in the outcome, a personal connection with those who suffer. The pressing urgency of the suffering would help them realize that something has to be done, and that their activities can play a vital part in solving the problem.

The would-be activist would have the opportunity to become acquainted with significant role models—people who are committed to justice and who are working to bring it into being. These role models would share not only their knowledge and skills but the passion and charisma of their commitment, and the vision of the human good that quickens their moral imagination.

They would be encouraged toward congruence between thought, feeling, and activity. An ethic of sociality would explain how involvement contributes to the good of the whole society, and thus to oneself as a member of that society. Would-be activists would be shown the difference between individual welfare efforts and action aimed at changing structures and institutions. They would learn not only about the interconnectedness of life, but about the effects and interconnectedness of individuals and systems. The scale of problems is too big and time is too short—problems must be addressed at the systemic level.

In their private life they would learn to be positive moral comparends to those around them and would bring critical reflection to bear on the institutions in their immediate life-world. This reflective practice would be supplemented with work at the level of public policy and a critique of the sustaining ethos of a culture.[1]

Each would learn the satisfaction of helping others. The kidney donors mentioned earlier in this study all reported a great sense of personal happiness at what they had done. It is also exciting to enter into the arenas of power—the places that make things happen. It is fun to win. It is even more fulfilling to know that one's activities can have an effect, that they can help not only one but perhaps thousands of other human beings. Social action need not flow from pure altruism. It can rise out of the satisfaction activism brings to the human quest for meaning. In loving a neighbor, one is loving oneself.

One final interview excerpt articulates some of these last points. Craig is an intelligent and insightful black who, had he chosen to be in banking, would in the upper echelons of money and power. Instead he chooses to invest his life in community service.

He describes himself as having a lot of pent-up misdirected energy in his youth that led to his being arrested and sent to the penitentiary. It was there just a few months before his release that a turning point occurred. He spent a lot of time talking with a fellow inmate about what to do when he got out of jail.

We'd rap and he suggested to me that he felt strongly that the secret to success was for an individual to come out of oneself in a cause or a project or a business.

That sounded good to Craig because he wanted to take his efforts and energies and direct them in some meaningful activity. He had been a house painter at one time, and that was not meaningful enough. And so:

By the time those gates opened and I caught that bus going home, it was almost like Moses going to the mountain top to visit the Lord, because I knew when that bus stopped exactly what I had to do. I had to go to college. I had to enter into sociology; I couldn't even spell sociology, didn't have any money—no money at all. But I knew what it was that I had to do. It was so clear to me because I knew I could achieve it. I was feeling good because I knew finally what to do with all those energies. I had a track to run on. And much of what I began doing from that point on had some meaning because I was doing it to prepare myself to help black folks. I finished a four-year college program in two and one-half years.

I think what I saw was the opportunity to do something that was needed and in so doing it provided me with some meaning. I don't believe people really do things for others out of some kind of altruistic bag. I think they do it because it is very personally satisfying. My involvement in the movement was done because it was very satisfying to me. It gave me a sense of well-being in the sense of accomplishment and achievement.

I'm convinced that those who deliberately come to the movement—whether you're talking about the Third World, black folk, poor people—as a volunteer it's not really real for you. But it's the individual I think who becomes totally immersed in whatever that cause is—now that doesn't mean that they have to be paid—but it means that whatever else they're doing is secondary, rather than their involvement as an afterthought or a part-time kind of thing.

Craig says "what I saw was the opportunity to do something that was needed and in so doing it provided me with some meaning." The quest for meaning is one of humankind's most enduring traits. The many places people find meaning is a testimonial to the versatility and creativity of the human imagination. Immersion in social change activity in behalf of the good society can bring a sense of meaning that is profound and lasting—even religious in its qualities.

I recall how a group of local citizens banded together some years ago to bring about some minor improvements in the local jail. The city council finally allocated money for hot meals, mattresses, and the posting of the jail rules in Spanish and English. Five years later I had occasion to go to that jail to get a friend released. There on the wall were those rules—helping me see how to proceed, just as they had helped thousands of people before and since that time. That experience was extraordinarily satisfying.

To shift to a larger scale, it is instructive to ask how many limbs and lives were saved because the Vietnam war was brought to a halt. Or to shift one more time to an even larger scale, how many lives and loves will be saved if we together prevent starvation and nuclear war? What sort of meaning would that provide those who make that happen?

Very early in this project I told John Howard Griffin about the research. "You want to know why people become involved?" he said. "I can tell you why. The roots lie in religion." (Late in life, Griffin had been working on a biography of Thomas Merton.)

If by religion one means identifiable church or synagogue, the evidence in the interviews is mixed indeed. Several of our participants said that although they had grown up in a strongly religious family, they now felt alienated from religious institutions. Sometimes the church seemed less moral than the political activists they encountered. The church's inaction on fundamental social issues was humanly and morally offensive to them. These people constitute a moral diaspora, the lost tribes. They were grounded in a religious tradition, but perhaps because of the values learned there, they are now alienated from its institutional manifestations.

Others among those interviewed continue to find their motivation, guidance, and strength in religious institutions. Among both religious and secular activists, one can find those who spend their entire lives working for justice, and might even be willing to die for it. This ultimate concern about people is itself a religious commitment.

It is fitting that this study, which began with John Howard Griffin's description of the suffering inside the rooms of Jews in Germany and blacks in America, should end with a quotation from Griffin, taken from an obituary article "Through Other Eyes," subtitled "John Howard Griffin's Life of Empathy." " 'The world,' Griffin once said, 'has always been saved by an Abrahamic minority. . . . There have always been a few who, in times of great trouble, became keenly aware of the underlying tragedy: the needless destruction of humanity.' "[2]

The world needs such an Abrahamic minority now, more than any other time in history. Each of us is invited to join with every other in the quest for justice—and in so doing, discover, create, and celebrate a meaningful world.

NOTES

Chapter 1

1. Husserl suggested that the *"first methodological principle"* is not to accept any judgment *"that I have not derived from evidence,* from 'experiences' in which the affairs and affair-complexes in question are present to me as *'they themselves.'* " Edmund Husserl, *Cartesian Meditations,* trans. Dorion Cairns (The Hague: Martinus Nijhoff, 1960), p. 13.
2. "Necessarily the point of departure is the object given 'straightforwardly' at the particular time. From it reflection goes back to the mode of consciousness at that time and to the potential modes of consciousness included horizonally in that mode, then to those in which the object might be otherwise intended as the same." Ibid., p. 50.
3. Carl Gustav Jung, *Erinnerungen, Träume, Gedanken* (Zürich: Rascher Verlag, 1962), p. 38 f., Spiegelberg's translation.
4. Herbert Spiegelberg, "On the 'I-Am-Me Experience' in Childhood and Adolescence," *Review of Existential Psychology and Psychiatry* 4.1 (February 1964):20.
5. Kenneth Keniston, *Young Radicals: Notes on Committed Youth* (New York: Harcourt Brace & World, 1968), pp. 133-146.

Chapter 2

1. Louis E. Raths, Merrill Harmin, and Sidney B. Simon, *Values and Teaching,* 2nd ed. (Columbus, Ohio: Charles E. Merrill Publishing Co., 1978), p. vii.
2. James Forman, *The Making of Black Revolutionaries* (New York: Macmillan Publishing Co., 1972), pp. 3-4.
3. Angelica Balabanoff, *My Life as a Rebel* (New York: Harper & Brothers, 1938; New York: Greenwood Press, 1968), p. 4.

Chapter 3

1. Paul Ricoeur, *Interpretation Theory: Discourse and the Surplus of Meaning* (Fort Worth, Texas: The Texas Christian University Press, 1976);

Hannah Arendt, *The Life of the Mind: Thinking* (New York: Harcourt Brace Jovanovich, 1978), vol. 1, p. 105; Ibid., p. 110; and H. Richard Niebuhr, *The Responsible Self* (New York: Harper & Row, 1963), p. 152.

2. Gaston Bachelard, *The Poetics of Space,* trans. from *La poétique de l'espace* by Maria Jolas (Presses Universitaires de France, 1958; Orion Press, 1964; Boston: Beacon Press, 1969), p. xi.

3. See especially Richard M. Zaner, *The Problem of Embodiment* (The Hague: Martinus Nijhoff, 1964).

4. Maulana Ron Karenga, quoted in James H. Cone, *Black Theology and Black Power* (New York: The Seabury Press, 1969), p. 32.

5. David Stewart and Algis Mickunas, *Exploring Phenomenology* (Chicago: American Library Association, 1974), pp. 96-99.

6. Ibid., p. 97.

7. Sheila D. Collins, *A Different Heaven and Earth* (Valley Forge, Pa.: Judson Press, 1974), pp. 177-182. See also Elizabeth Dodson Gray, *Green Paradise Lost* (Wellesley, Mass.: Roundtable Press, 1979), pp. 109-117.

8. Edmund Husserl spoke of descriptive analysis and constitutional analysis. In the first, "one explicates objective moments of the object, its qualities, its relations to other objects. In constitutional analysis one considers the act in which the objects and the objective moments are given." "Conversation with Husserl, 28/8/31," Dorion Cairns, *Conversations with Husserl and Fink* (The Hague: Martinus Nijhoff, 1976), pp. 27-28.

9. Talcott Parsons and Edward A. Shils, eds., *Toward a General Theory of Action* (Cambridge, Mass.: Harvard University Press, 1951; New York: Harper & Row, Torchbooks, 1962), p. 4ff. Erving Goffman, *Frame Analysis* (New York: Harper & Row, Harper Colophon, 1974).

10. Edward A. Tiryakian, "Sociology and Existential Phenomenology" in *Phenomenology and the Social Sciences,* ed. Maurice Natanson (Evanston, Ill.: Northwestern University Press, 1973), 1:199.

11. Gibson Winter suggests that the ethos of Western culture has moved from a paradigm based on an organic metaphor to one based on a mechanist metaphor. He proposes a new guiding paradigm of artistic process as creativity. Gibson Winter, *Liberating Creation* (New York: The Crossroad Publishing Co., 1981), pp. 2-6, 105-15.

12. Peter L. Berger and Thomas Luckmann, *The Social Construction of Reality* (New York: Doubleday & Co., Anchor Books, 1966), p. 137.

13. George Procter-Smith, Richard A. Hoehn, and Marjorie Procter-Smith, "People of Vision" (manuscript), p. 17. This manuscript uses phenomenological categories to examine the life-world of selected persons and groups in the Christian tradition who help a radical vision of the [Christian and] human good.

14. Lincoln Steffens, *The Autobiography of Lincoln Steffens* (New York: Harcourt, Brace & Co., 1931).

15. Ibid., p. 238.

16. Richard M. Zaner, *The Way of Phenomenology* (Indianapolis, Ind.: The Bobbs-Merrill Co., Pegasus, 1970), p. 47.

17. Monica B. Morris, *An Excursion into Creative Sociology* (New York: Columbia University Press, 1977), p. 129.

18. Steffens, *The Autobiography of,* pp. 369-70.

19. Ibid., p. 479.

20. Ibid., p. 434.

21. Tiryakian, "Sociology and Existential Phenomenology," p. 202.

22. Mike Ritchey, "Where Have All the Activists Gone?" *Prime Time* 6:10 (August 1977):9.

23. Edgar H. Schein with Inge Schneier and Curtis H. Barker, *Coercive Persuasion,* Center for International Studies, Massachusetts Institute of Technology (New York: W. W. Norton & Co., 1961), pp. 119-20.
24. Robert Jay Lifton, *Thought Reform and the Psychology of Totalism* (New York: W. W. Norton & Co., 1961), p. 463.
25. Robert Jay Lifton, *Home From the War* (New York: Simon & Schuster, 1973), p. 16.
26. Ibid., p. 46.
27. Ibid., pp. 53, 56.
28. Thomas S. Kuhn, *The Structure of Scientific Revolutions* (1962; reprint, Chicago: University of Chicago Press, Phoenix Books, 1964), p. 10.
29. Ibid., pp. 52-53.
30. Ibid., pp. 84-85.
31. Ibid., p. 64.
32. Ibid., p. 84.

Chapter 4

1. Peter Berger, *Invitation to Sociology* (New York: Doubleday & Co., Anchor Books, 1963), pp. 51-52.
2. Berger and Luckmann, *The Social Construction of Reality,* p. 157.
3. Ibid., p. 157.
4. Dag Hammarskjöld, *Markings,* trans. Leif Sjöberg and W. H. Auden (New York: Alfred A. Knopf, 1964), p. 144.
5. Bachelard, *The Poetics of Space,* p. 8.
6. Stanley Milgram, *Obedience to Authority* (1974; reprint, New York: Harper & Row, Harper Colophon, 1975), p. 34.
7. Nicolai Hartmann, *Ethics,* vol. 1, *Moral Phenomena,* Stanton Coit, trans., with an introduction by J. H. Muirhead (London: George Allen & Unwin; New York: Macmillan Co., 1932), pp. 41-42.
8. Tiryakian, "Sociology and Existential Phenomenology," p. 200.
9. For the examples cited here and a summary of other studies, see Ted L. Huston and Chuck Korte, "The Responsive Bystander: Why He Helps," in *Moral Development and Behavior,* ed. Thomas Lickona (New York: Holt, Rinehart, & Winston, 1976), pp. 269-283.
10. Albert Camus, *The Stranger,* trans. Stuart Gilbert (New York: Alfred A. Knopf, 1946; New York: Random House, Vintage Books, 1954), pp. 99-100.
11. Robert C. Solomon, *The Passions* (1976; reprint, New York: Doubleday & Co., Anchor Books, 1977), p. 186.
12. Ibid., p. 212.
13. Ibid., pp. 252, 213.

Chapter 5

1. Keniston, *Young Radicals,* p. 133.
2. Perry London, "The Rescuers: Motivational Hypotheses About Christians Who Saved Jews From the Nazis," in *Altruism and Helping Behavior,* ed. J. Macaulay and L. Berkowitz (New York: Academic Press, 1970), pp. 241-250.
3. See Huston and Korte, "The Responsive Bystander," pp. 269-283.
4. Keniston, *Young Radicals,* pp. 140-141.
5. London, "The Rescuers," p. 245.

6. Huston and Korte, "The Responsive Bystander," p. 273.
7. John M. Darley and C. Daniel Batson, " 'From Jerusalem to Jericho': A Study of Situational and Dispositional Variables in Helping Behavior," *Journal of Personality and Social Psychology* 27:1 (1973): 100-108.
8. Ibid., p. 104.
9. Ibid., p. 107.
10. Huston and Korte, "The Responsive Bystander," p. 273.
11. Alfred Schutz, *Collected Papers*, vol. 1, *The Problem of Social Reality*, ed. and intro. by Maurice Natanson (The Hague: Martinus Nijhoff, 1967), pp. 306-307. See also Alfred Schutz and Thomas Luckmann, *The Structures of the Life-World*, trans. Richard M. Zaner and H. Tristram Englehardt, Jr. (Evanston, Ill.: Northwestern University Press, 1973), pp. 41-43.
12. Zaner, *The Problem of Embodiment*, pp. 23-24.
13. Ibid., p. 96.
14. Schutz, *Collected Papers*, 1:307; and Schutz and Luckmann, *Structures of the Life World*, p. 42.
15. Keniston, *Young Radicals*, p. 133.
16. See Richard McKeon, "The Development and the Significance of the Concept of Responsibility," *Revue Internationale de Philosophie* 11:39 (1957):3-32.
17. Hans Jonas, "The Concept of Responsibility," in *Knowledge, Value and Belief*, ed. H. Tristram Englehardt, Jr., and Daniel Callahan (Hastings-on-Hudson, New York: Institute of Society, Ethics and the Life Sciences, 1977), pp. 170-171.
18. Milgram, *Obedience to Authority*, pp. 32-43.
19. Dorothy Day, *The Long Loneliness* (New York: Harper & Brothers, 1952), p. 38.
20. Huston and Korte, "The Responsive Bystander," p. 273.
21. Alexander Pfänder, *Phenomenology of Willing and Motivation*, trans. and intro. by Herbert Spiegelberg (Evanston, Ill.: Northwestern University Press, 1967), p. 15.
22. Peter Schrag, "The Ellsberg Affair," *Saturday Review* 54:46 (November 13, 1971), p. 35.
23. Carl H. Fellner and John R. Marshall, "Kidney Donors," in *Altruism and Helping Behavior*, p. 272.
24. Margaret Sanger, *An Autobiography* (New York: W. W. Norton & Co., 1938; Elmsford, New York: Maxwell Reprint Co., 1970), p. 89.
25. Ibid., p. 91.
26. Ibid., pp. 91-92.
27. Ibid., p. 92.

Chapter 6

1. Procter-Smith, Hoehn, Procter-Smith, "People of Vision," p. 214.
2. Tiryakian, "Sociology and Existential Phenomenology," p. 212.
3. David Rosenhan, "The Natural Socialization of Altruistic Autonomy," in *Altruism and Helping Behavior*, p. 263.
4. Ibid., p. 267.
5. Keniston, *Young Radicals*, pp. 135-40.
6. Milgram, *Obedience to Authority*, pp. 59-62.
7. Herbert C. Kelman and Lee H. Lawrence, "Assignment of Responsibility in the Case of Lt. Calley," *Journal of Social Issues* 28.1 (1972), pp. 192-94.

8. Ibid., p. 194.

9. Robert L. Heilbroner, *An Inquiry into the Human Prospect* (New York: W. W. Norton & Co., 1974), p. 111.

10. Adam Smith, *The Theory of Moral Sentiments* (London, 1759; new ed., London: Henry G. Bohn, 1853; reprint, New York: Augustus M. Kelley, Publishers, 1966), p. 4.

11. Max Scheler, *The Nature of Sympathy,* trans. Peter Heath (Hamden, Conn.: The Shoe String Press, Archon Books, 1970), pp. 49-50.

12. Ibid.

13. Max Scheler, *Formalism in Ethics and Non-Formal Ethics of Values,* trans. Manfred S. Frings and Roger L. Funk (Evanston, Ill.: Northwestern University Press, 1973), p. 255.

14. A. R. Luther, *Persons in Love: A Study of Max Scheler's Wesen und Formen der Sympathie* (The Hague: Martinus Nijhoff, 1972), pp. 87-88.

15. Philip M. Boffey, "Strategy of War Reclines on Psychologist's Couch," *Fort Worth Star-Telegram,* New York Times News Service, 7 September 1982, pp. 1-2.

16. Ibid.

17. Ibid.

18. Procter-Smith, Hoehn, Procter-Smith, "People of Vision," pp. 15-16.

Chapter 7

1. Franz Kafka, *I Am a Memory Come Alive,* ed. Nahum H. Glatzer (New York: Schocken Books, 1974), pp. vii-viii.

2. Henri Bergson, *Matter and Memory,* trans. by Nancy Margaret Paul and W. Scott Palmer (London: George Allen & Unwin, 1911), p. 80.

3. ". . . the phenomenological concept of so-called 'articulated' or 'polythetic' syntheses, namely those in which discrete, discontinuous acts of experiencing are bound together in an articulated unity, in the unity of a synthetic act of a higher order. It is the peculiarity of such polythetic syntheses that consciousness can grasp their step-by-step formation only in a 'fan of several rays of thought,' whereas the integrated object, once synthesized, can be experienced in one single ray of thought, in a 'monothetic' act." Alfred Schutz, *Collected Papers,* ed. I. Schutz (The Hague: Martinus Nijhoff, 1970), 3:13. Schutz was connecting this polythetic-monothetic concept with William James' description of a train of thought in which " 'The practical upshot of a book we read remains with us, though we may not recall one of its sentences.' " Ibid.

4. Solomon, *The Passions,* p. 79.

5. Ibid., p. 277.

6. Peter L. Berger, *Pyramids of Sacrifice* (New York: Basic Books, Publishers, 1974), p. 17.

7. Gibson Winter, "A Language of Religious Social Ethics" (manuscript), IV.20.

8. Donald M. Lowe, "Intentionality and the Method of History," in *Phenomenology and the Social Sciences,* ed. Maurice Natanson (Evanston, Ill.: Northwestern University Press, 1973), 2:123.

9. William Earle, *The Autobiographical Consciousness* (Chicago: Quadrangle Books, 1972), p. 160.

10. Solomon, *The Passions,* p. 277.

Chapter 8

1. For an exposition of ethos, public policy, and reflective practice, see Alvin Pitcher and Gibson Winter, "Perspectives in Religious Social Ethics," *Journal of Religious Ethics* 5.1 (1977): 69-89.

2. Robert Ellsberg, "Through Other Eyes," *Sojourners* (February 1981), p. 22.

INDEX

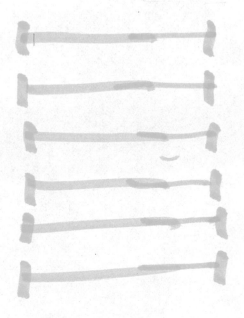

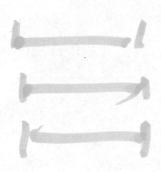